MORE PRAISE FOR

Clean Treats for Everyone

"Laura proves that you can stick to your health goals without feeling deprived! Laura's recipes have always been foolproof and I'm so glad I can eat and share treats that are not only healthy but also delicious!"

—Amy Roskelley, owner of Health Beet

"*Clean Treats for Everyone* is a must-have for anyone who loves desserts but doesn't love highly processed ingredients. Laura will teach you how to stock your pantry and swap ingredients to make delicious treats without all the junk. Finally, a cookbook full of clean treat recipes that pacifies my sweet tooth and I can feel good about making for my kids!"

—Kelley Epstein, from MountainMamaCooks.com

LAURA FUENTES

CLEAN TREATS

for Everyone

Healthy Desserts and Snacks Made with
Simple, Real Food Ingredients

FAIR WINDS

Inspiring | Educating | Creating | Entertaining

Brimming with creative inspiration, how-to projects, and useful information to enrich your everyday life, Quarto Knows is a favorite destination for those pursuing their interests and passions. Visit our site and dig deeper with our books into your area of interest: Quarto Creates, Quarto Cooks, Quarto Homes, Quarto Lives, Quarto Drives, Quarto Explores, Quarto Gifts, or Quarto Kids.

First Published in 2020 by Fair Winds Press, an imprint of The Quarto Group,
100 Cummings Center, Suite 265-D, Beverly, MA 01915, USA.
T (978) 282-9590 F (978) 283-2742 QuartoKnows.com

Fair Winds Press titles are also available at discount for retail, wholesale, promotional, and bulk purchase. For details, contact the Special Sales Manager by email at specialsales@quarto.com or by mail at The Quarto Group, Attn: Special Sales Manager, 100 Cummings Center, Suite 265-D, Beverly, MA 01915, USA.

24 23 22 21 20   1 2 3 4 5

ISBN: 978-1-59233-964-8

Digital edition published in 2020

Library of Congress Cataloging-in-Publication Data

Library of Congress Control Number: 2020936823

Design: Kate Barraclough (Kate Frances Design)
Cover Image: Alison Bickel Photography
Page Layout: Kate Barraclough (Kate Frances Design)
Photography: Alison Bickel Photography

Printed in China

The information in this book is for educational purposes only. It is not intended to replace the advice of a physician or medical practitioner. Please see your healthcare provider before beginning any new health program.

To my kids, Sofia, Alex, and Gabriel.

Your sweet tooth challenges this mama to make treats that taste "real."

Contents

Introduction

"If you eat your veggies you can have a treat" are words spoken by many parents, mid-meal, trying to get their kids to eat their food. "But it's good for you!" is often another plea we all have made to our children.

I know this scenario well because I've lived it with all three of my kids. And while veggies are not my kids' favorite thing to eat, treats certainly are. "I don't want to eat a cookie," said no child ever. Right?

I've been developing whole-food, real-ingredient, and clean-eating recipes for MOMables.com, LauraFuentes.com, and all of my cookbooks since 2010, and my family has been the unpaid test group for most of my work before I consider publishing it.

With the exception of my second cookbook, *The Best Homemade Kids' Snacks on the Planet*, most of my recipes have focused on the main meal, providing solutions for breakfast, lunch, and dinner, as well as an entire cookbook dedicated to tacos!

And while all of the recipes have been tremendously well received by my community, one thing I'm often asked is "Do you have any recipes for clean treats I can feel good about eating?"

Of course, I have them. I just rarely share them. No, they aren't a secret for me to keep; on the contrary, I publish my best stuff for everyone to make. The truth is that the thought of publishing treats never occurred to me, even though I test and modify recipes I come across the internet almost weekly to fit our dietary needs.

In 2018, I launched the *Family KickStart Program* at MOMables.com, where parents can eliminate processed foods and added sugars from their family's diet and reset the way they eat as a family. And while the thirty-day program has been very successful for thousands of families, one piece of feedback I received from parents was to include more occasional treats for their family to enjoy.

You could say that I finally heard the universe telling me to create, write, and share simple clean treat recipes families can enjoy and not feel guilty about eating!

The recipes you see in this book are just that: crave-worthy treats you can make with simple ingredients you already have in your pantry.

CHAPTER ONE

The Basics of Clean Eating and Baking

—

"Make the right choices, no matter how you eat" was my friend Kelly's advice to me when I asked her what eating "clean" meant. Kelly is a registered dietitian who focuses on whole-food family nutrition and often asks me for tips and shortcuts when it comes to real-food cooking.

For many years, she's shared my cookbooks and online recipes with her clients, since my approach has always been to use real-food ingredients in simple everyday recipes.

For the purposes of this book, the treat recipes avoid ingredients that are highly processed; meaning, that they are so far from nature that they lack any nutrition. This includes ready-made mixes and items with preservative-filled, mystery ingredients.

When it comes to using a sweetener for the treats in this cookbook, I've chosen to test and create recipes with honey, maple syrup, and coconut palm sugar. Coconut sugar also contains zinc and calcium, plus antioxidants and probiotics. So, for these reasons, along with the fact that it's unrefined, I've chosen it as the replacement for granulated (white and brown) sugar in this cookbook; it's my favorite clean sweetener to use.

This is not a sugar-free cookbook, however. It's a desserts cookbook that includes recipes made with clean ingredients. Of course, ingredients will always vary by brand, such as the case with chocolate chips. So make sure to check the label whenever possible.

When it comes to clean meals, it's easy to follow a recipe and stick with a plan. The key word: *plan*. But when the craving for something sweet sets in, it's tempting to grab a candy bar while waiting at the check-out line or to throw a box of cookies in the grocery cart.

I hope the recipes in this cookbook help you avoid purchasing convenient, processed desserts while letting you enjoy a sweet treat from time to time with your family and friends.

What to Expect from This Book

When I shared some of the recipes I wanted to include in this book with Kelly, her response was an exciting one: "I wish I had these recipes on hand for the last decade to share with my clients! One of the things they miss the most are treats. Hurry up and get the book published!"

While our journeys to a clean-eating diet

might look a little different, we all have the same need for deliciously simple treats that will be devoured by adults and kids alike. The recipes in this book are the ones I make for family and bring to playdates and celebrations, and I'm proud to share them with you.

Clean Eating + Gluten-Free

One of the non-negotiables when it came to developing recipes for this book was making sure that every recipe could be enjoyed gluten-free.

While whole-wheat flour is considered to be "clean" by many, I know that a lot of people in my community already follow a gluten-free diet due to allergies, intolerances, autoimmune conditions, and personal preference.

There are other whole grains that are also clean that were not included in this book. The only grain I included in a couple of recipes was oats, because it's both easily available and naturally gluten-free. *It goes without saying that if you suffer from celiac disease you should purchase oats that are clearly labeled gluten-free to avoid cross contamination.*

It's safe to say that the recipes in this book are naturally gluten-free simply by the ingredients used. However, make sure to check the labels of the ingredients since some facilities use the same equipment to process both wheat and gluten-free products. Items that are made in gluten-free facilities usually include the gluten-free seal of approval on the packaging.

Clean Eating + Dairy-Free

Nearly all recipes in this book are dairy-free and suitable for a dairy-free diet. The most significant hidden source of dairy is chocolate.

You might have noticed that there are a lot of chocolate recipes in this book, so if a dairy-free diet is a requirement for you and your family's health, please check the label in the packaging. There are many dairy-free brands for chocolate chips available both at traditional grocery stores and online.

For this reason, the recipes that are already dairy-free but contain chocolate chips or chunks, for example, are marked as dairy-free. I assume that you will be purchasing ingredients that are safe to consume for you and your family.

If you can tolerate dairy, you can use:
- ♥ Cow's milk instead of almond milk
- ♥ Half and half (equal parts whole milk and light cream) instead of coconut milk
- ♥ Butter (melted) instead of coconut oil
- ♥ Traditional chocolate chips versus dairy-free chocolate chips

Clean Eating + Nut-Free

This book contains nuts and seeds in some recipes. The recipes that require almond flour were included because they yielded the best texture, when tested.

Like in my cookbook *The Best Grain-Free Family Meals on the Planet*, I've felt strongly about making sure that nearly all recipes included in the book were tested with a nut-free option, not just for your family's safety but also for the safety of other children with severe nut allergies around your child.

If you have nut allergies or are bringing these treats to a school, I highly suggest using oat flour in a 1:1 ratio to replace the almond flour in the recipes. Check out page 17 to learn how to make oat flour.

The Shopping List: How to Stock Your Pantry with Clean Ingredients

The main requirement during recipe development was for the ingredients in all recipes to be clean and unprocessed. After that, I wanted the ingredients to be available at most grocery stores, not just on Amazon. Better yet would be if they were already inside most pantries of people who were trying to eat clean.

If you are looking to "clean up" the baking shelf in your pantry, below you'll find a list of ingredients I keep in my pantry and kitchen at all times that make whipping up the recipes in this book possible.

I purchase many of these items in bulk, both online and at a wholesale membership store, and they are typically stored in my pantry, at room temperature, in airtight containers or sealed bags. Some, like almond flour, do best in the refrigerator or freezer.

Tip:

Raw nuts and seeds can be stored in the freezer, and nut and seed butters in the refrigerator, to extend their shelf life.

Nuts and Seeds
Almond butter
Almonds
Cashews
Chia seeds
Flax seeds (whole or ground)
Peanut butter
Pecans
Pumpkin seeds
Sunflower seeds
Tahini
Walnuts

Flours and Grains
Almond flour
Coconut flour
Oat flour
Oats
Tapioca starch

Clean Fats
Butter
Coconut oil
Ghee
Olive oil

Baking Staples
Baking powder
Baking soda
Blanched almond flour or almond meal
Coconut milk, full fat (canned)
Chocolate chips (check the ingredients of traditional brands)
Dried fruits
Unsweetened cocoa powder or cacao powder
Unsweetened coconut flakes and shredded coconut
Vanilla extract

Natural Sweeteners
Coconut palm sugar
Dried fruits (no added sugar)
Honey
Maple syrup
Pitted dates
Raisins

Fresh Ingredients
Apples
Bananas
Berries
Carrots
Citrus
Oranges
Watermelon
Zucchini

Other Pantry Items
Ground cinnamon
Ground flax or flax seeds
Matcha powder
Pumpkin purée
Turmeric powder

All Other Allergy Restrictions

I can't possibly account for all the different individual-ingredient allergies out there. Soy is also a big allergen and all the recipes in this book are free of soy.

The next biggest food allergy that would prevent you from enjoying some of the recipes in this book is eggs. While rare, egg allergies exist and can be a hindrance for some of the recipes included.

When recipes call for fewer than 2 eggs, you can use a "flax egg" substitute. See page 17 for the recipe.

At the top of each recipe you'll find the following simple icons to help you navigate a recipe and decide whether you'll need to make any adjustments for allergies or intolerances. At a glance, you'll know whether the recipe fits within your dietary restrictions.

- **GF** **gluten-free**
- **DF** **dairy-free**
- **EF** **egg-free**
- **NF** **nut-free**
- **V** **vegan**

What's the Difference Between Coconut Milk and Coconut Cream?

You'll find both in a can or a plastic pack, but what's the real difference?

Coconut milk has the consistency of whole cow's milk and yogurt. It's made from equal parts shredded coconut and water. Because some separation occurs, a quick shake of the can or blending before using should homogenize the consistency.

Made from four parts shredded coconut and one part water, coconut cream is thicker and richer than coconut milk in both flavor and texture.

Kitchen Gadgets for Baking

One of the things you'll notice in this book, compared to most dessert books, is that the recipes are made using standard size pans and baking sheets as well as common kitchen tools such as a blender and a whisk.

There are a couple of recipes, however, that call for a springform pan; and truth be told, I had to purchase one when I set out to create the cheesecake recipes. If you're thinking "I'll just skip those," do yourself a favor and buy the $8 pan because the Chocolate Cheesecake (see page 116) is the best you'll ever make (more than once).

Do you really need an ice cream maker? Yes, you most absolutely do if you want a creamy consistency to the ice cream recipes in this book. I tried to make them with a "no-churn" method but the texture was most often icy and not the same achieved from an ice cream maker. I bought mine online for less than $40 and I've used it hundreds of times.

Food Processor versus Blender, or Both

Many recipes in this book can be made in either a blender or food processor. When a recipe yields better results with one of the two, you'll see it as the appliance used.

Hand Mixer versus Stand Mixer

My stand mixer is about two decades young and it's always on the counter at the Studio (my film

How to Make Oat Flour

Yield: approximately 1 ½ cups (100 g) oat flour

Oat flour can easily be made in a blender or food processor. The key to even textured baked goods is making sure the oats are ground powdery fine. You can use old fashioned (large flakes) or quick-cooking oats to make oat flour. The yield is approximately 1 cup (80 g) oats for every ¾ cup (75 g) oat flour. Consider making extra and keeping a ready-ground canister of oat flour in your fridge or freezer for future use. For best results, let the oat flour warm up to room temperature prior to using.

Place 2 cups (160 g) oats inside the blender or food processor. Blend or process until smooth.

How to Make a Flax Egg

To make a "flax egg," use 1 tablespoon (7 g) ground flax and 3 tablespoons (45 ml) warm water.

In a small bowl, combine the ground flax and the warm water. Wait 10 minutes for the mixture to become gel-like and then use in the recipe in place of an egg. This "flax egg" works for most cookies, breads, and bars with fewer than 2 eggs.

How to Make Whipped Coconut Cream

Yield: approximately 1 ½ cups (180 g)

As you look through the recipes you'll find many of them are served with whipped coconut cream, a dairy-free alternative to regular whipped cream. While it's easy to make, you'll need to use the actual coconut cream solids. This is most easily done with a refrigerated can of coconut cream, because refrigeration allows the fats to solidify and makes it easy to separate from the liquid.

14-ounce (403 ml) can coconut cream or full-fat coconut milk, refrigerated overnight
1 teaspoon honey

Scoop the cream from the top of the can into a large chilled bowl, making sure all of the liquid remains in the can.

Using a hand mixer or stand mixer, beat the cream on high; add the honey. Continue beating until stiff peaks form, around 2 to 3 minutes.

kitchen). At home, I have a hand mixer, so I use that. There's no need to purchase another large appliance, since all the recipes can successfully be made with both.

Baking Pans

The recipes in this book will always call out the size of the pan needed to yield the best results. Rectangular and square baking pans are typically glass; loaf pans can be glass or metal; and baking sheets are metal. Cupcake/muffin pans are both standard size and mini. The standard size muffin pan has twelve spaces and the mini muffin pan has twenty-four.

Parchment Paper

Many recipes in this book call for the use of parchment paper when lining a baking pan. You can use a silicone mat instead, although I recommend you keep a roll of parchment paper handy for rolling out dough and lining baking pans for easy lifting. I personally use both.

Healthier Swaps: The Best Ingredients to Make Clean Treats

The recipes in this cookbook were created to fully satisfy a sweet tooth. It would be great if in every recipe oil could be substituted with applesauce and yield a great treat. It's very difficult for healthier options to mimic how butter or oil can soften a cookie or make brownies fudgy—they just can't!

I'm sure you're wondering if there's a difference between healthy treats and clean treats. There's a reason this cookbook is called *Clean Treats* and not *Healthy Treats*. This is because the word "healthy" can mean a lot of different things for different people and it's

nearly impossible to make everyone happy.

You know what makes me happy? Treats made with real-food ingredients that are minimally processed or not at all, which is why I chose to focus on the ingredient aspect (clean) and not the dietary preference (healthy) of a recipe.

The most important factor to consider when making substitutions is texture. Can you replace honey with maple syrup? Yes, because both are liquid sweeteners. Can you replace coconut sugar with honey? Not always. Can you reduce the sweetener content in a recipe by simply cutting the measurement in half? Sometimes.

As someone whose recipes are made by millions of people each year, I always advise that when you take it upon yourself to make substitutions and deviate from the recipe as written, I can't guarantee its successful outcome.

I use coconut flour throughout this book because it's high in fiber, low in carbohydrates, and quite nutritious. Coconut "flour" is made from unsweetened and dehydrated coconut that has been ground until it has achieved a flour-like texture. *Unfortunately, it does not behave like traditional flour, so it can't be substituted with almond, oat, or any other flour.* The recipes that call for coconut flour stand in a league of their own and are worth making. The great news is that coconut flour is easy to find at the store and in bulk online.

At the end of the day, baking is an art and a science. As beautiful and delicious as the recipes are inside this book, more time has gone into developing the right ratios for best results.

The recipes in this book are designed to guide you in your journey to a cleaner diet. I hope they inspire you to add variety in your family's treats as much as they've helped me with mine.

CHAPTER TWO

Oven-Fresh Treats

From bakery-style muffins to naturally sweetened bars and cookies, you'll find recipes to cover everything from breakfast to after-dinner treats in this chapter. Bonus: Many of these recipes are simple enough for kids to help with too!

—

Batter Be Good

MUFFINS, BROWNIES, CAKES, AND BREADS

Cranberry Orange Muffins

These are my favorite muffins to make during the holidays when cranberries are abundant, and I go overly zealous in purchasing them. Since they store in the freezer for a long time, you'll find me making a batch of these muffins also in mid-March (seriously). The fresh cranberries and fresh orange zest give these muffins the holiday flavors we all love, and their scent will fill your home. With a hearty texture, they are just the kind of muffin that I enjoy eating while I sip a cup of coffee.

Yield: 8 muffins

———

2 cups (240 g) oat flour
½ cup (40 g) rolled oats
1 teaspoon orange zest
1 teaspoon baking soda
¼ teaspoon salt
½ cup (120 ml) melted coconut oil
2 large eggs
⅓ cup (115 g) honey
1 teaspoon vanilla extract
½ cup (120 ml) fresh orange juice
1 cup (105 g) fresh cranberries

Preheat oven to 350°F (180°C) and line a 12-count muffin pan with 8 paper liners.

In a medium bowl, combine the oat flour, oats, orange zest, baking soda, and salt. Stir to combine.

In a separate large bowl, combine the coconut oil, eggs, honey, vanilla extract, and orange juice; whisk to combine.

Working in batches, add the dry ingredients to the wet ingredients, stirring to combine after each addition, until smooth. Fold in the cranberries.

Fill each muffin liner to about ¾ full. Bake for 16 minutes or until a toothpick comes out clean when inserted in the middle.

Remove from the oven and allow muffins to cool down before removing from the pan.

Chocolate Mug Cake

There I was, sitting on the couch at almost midnight while everyone slept, craving chocolate. We were out of eggs—not something that happens often at my house—and then I remembered my friend Jenna's egg-free (she's allergic to eggs) "Break-up Cake" we ate from a mug years earlier, as she sobbed over her ex.

Thankfully, I fired up a text: "I NEED YOUR BREAKUP MUG CAKE RECIPE NOW!" And as fast as the request went out, in came the recipe.

This simple mug cake satisfies all the chocolate cravings, and it's made for one so you don't have to share.

   GF DF EF V

Yield: 1 serving

———

2 tablespoons (14 g) oat flour

1 tablespoon (7 g) unsweetened cocoa powder

2 teaspoons (8 g) coconut sugar

¼ teaspoon baking powder

⅛ teaspoon salt

1 tablespoon (15 ml) melted coconut oil

2 tablespoons (30 ml) unsweetened almond milk

1 tablespoon (16 g) almond butter

1 tablespoon (10 g) chocolate chips

———

For this recipe to be dairy-free, use allergy-friendly chocolate chips.

In a large mug, combine the oat flour, cocoa powder, sugar, baking powder, and salt. Stir until there are no clumps.

Stir in the coconut oil and milk until the mixture is smooth. Drop a tablespoon of almond butter into the center and push it down into the batter.

Sprinkle the chocolate chips over the mug cake and microwave on high for 1 minute.

Remove and enjoy.

Chocolate Cake

No treats cookbook would be complete without a chocolate cake recipe, and this one is over the top! Whipped coconut chocolate frosting was a total genius move for this recipe—after one bite I promise you won't miss the bakery's or boxed version, because this is the real deal!

Yield: 9 servings

½ cup (67 g) coconut flour
¼ cup (28 g) almond flour
2 teaspoons (8 g) baking
  powder
½ cup (60 g) unsweetened
  cocoa powder
14-ounce (403 ml) can full-fat
  coconut milk
½ cup (170 g) maple syrup
4 large eggs
2 teaspoons (10 ml) vanilla
  extract

Chocolate Frosting
1 cup (175 g) dark chocolate
  chunks
¼ cup (60 ml) full-fat canned
  coconut milk
¼ cup (60 ml) coconut oil

---

*For this recipe to be dairy-free,
use allergy-friendly chocolate
chunks.*

Preheat oven to 350°F (180°C). Line a 9 × 9-inch (23 × 23 cm) square baking pan with parchment paper.

Combine the coconut flour, almond flour, baking powder, and cocoa powder in the bowl of a stand mixer (or large mixing bowl). Mix on low speed until combined.

In a high-speed blender, combine the coconut milk, maple syrup, eggs, and vanilla extract. Blend on low speed for 10 to 15 seconds until all ingredients are thoroughly combined.

With your stand mixer on low speed, slowly pour wet ingredients into dry. Mix just enough for everything to combine; do not overmix the batter. It should look like a chocolate mousse.

Pour the batter into the prepared pan and bake for 50 minutes or until a toothpick comes out clean when inserted in the middle.

Allow the cake to cool completely before lifting the edges of the parchment paper to remove the cake from the pan.

While the cake bakes, in a double boiler melt the frosting ingredients over medium heat. Whisk until smooth and completely combined.

Transfer the frosting to the freezer for 15 to 30 minutes.

Remove the frosting from the freezer and use a hand mixer to whip the frosting until stiff peaks form. Spread the frosting over the cake, slice, and serve.

Store leftovers in the fridge for up to a week.

Chocolate Chunk Brownies

Making homemade brownies is very satisfying. There's the mixing of the ingredients in the bowl, the aroma emitted from the oven that begins to fill the kitchen once the chocolate begins to bake . . . oh yes! Let's not forget about licking the spatula. That's what everyone in my family fights over.

These chunky chocolate brownies are love at first bite. The chocolate chunks freshly chopped off a chocolate block for this recipe, provide a chocolatey surprise for your taste buds.

Yield: 12 servings

½ cup (125 g) almond butter
¼ cup (60 ml) melted
   coconut oil
¾ cup (135 g) coconut sugar
1 large egg
1 tablespoon (15 ml) vanilla
   extract
1 cup (118 g) almond flour
½ cup (60 g) unsweetened
   cocoa powder
1 teaspoon baking soda
½ teaspoon salt
4 ounces (115 g) dark chocolate,
   coarsely chopped

---

*For this recipe to be dairy-free,
use allergy-friendly chocolate
chips.*

Preheat oven to 350°F (180°C). Line a 9 x 9-inch (23 cm x 23 cm) square baking pan with parchment paper.

In a large bowl, combine the almond butter, coconut oil, coconut sugar, egg, and vanilla extract until smooth. Stir in the almond flour, cocoa powder, baking soda, and salt. Fold in the chocolate pieces to evenly distribute into the dough.

Transfer the batter to the prepared pan and bake for 20 minutes or until lightly browned.

Remove from oven and allow to cool before slicing into 12 squares.

Fudgy Chocolate Brownies

My second intern and now close friend Monica shared this recipe years ago and it has been my go-to brownie recipe ever since. We used to joke about the simplicity of the recipe, how they were "good for you because of the eggs providing protein and the cocoa's antioxidants!" Well, I love them so much I had to ask her if I could include it in my cookbook and share them with you.

These brownies are perfectly moist, soft, and fudgy without being undercooked and feeling like you are eating chocolate fudge. They are not fudge. They are like biting into a moist chocolate cloud.

What I love about this recipe is that they are flourless, so I don't have to make oat flour or worry about nut allergies or gluten-free needs when I make them for a crowd. Monica makes hers with olive oil, but I prefer using coconut oil or butter (when I don't have to omit dairy) instead.

Yield: 8 servings

4 large eggs

1 cup (120 g) unsweetened cocoa powder

⅓ cup (115 g) honey or maple syrup

⅓ cup (70 ml) melted coconut oil

2 teaspoons (10 ml) vanilla extract

Preheat the oven to 350°F (180°C). Line a 4 x 8-inch (10 cm x 20 cm) loaf pan.

In a large bowl, combine the eggs, cocoa powder, honey or maple syrup, coconut oil, and vanilla extract; whisk until smooth.

Pour the batter into the loaf pan and bake for 18 to 20 minutes or until a toothpick comes out clean when inserted in the center.

Remove from oven and allow to cool for 10 minutes before slicing into 8 squares.

Lemon Loaf

Mimicking my daughter's favorite lemon loaf at the famous coffee house, this quick bread is super moist and refreshing. It's also a lot cheaper than our usual order and it's made with ingredients I feel good about eating.

Yield: 1 loaf

---

1 ½ cups (170 g) oat flour
½ cup (57 g) almond flour
1 teaspoon baking powder
1 teaspoon baking soda
½ teaspoon salt
2 eggs
¼ cup (60 ml) melted
  coconut oil
½ cup (170 g) honey
¼ cup (60 ml) almond milk
1 teaspoon vanilla extract
½ cup (120 ml) lemon juice
1 teaspoon lemon zest

Sweet Glaze
1 tablespoon (15 ml) lemon juice
1 tablespoon (15 ml) honey
1 tablespoon (15 ml) almond
  milk
½ teaspoon vanilla extract
2 tablespoons (30 ml) coconut
  oil

Preheat oven to 350°F (180°C) and line an 8 x 4-inch (20 cm x 10 cm) loaf pan with parchment paper.

In a medium bowl, combine the oat flour, almond flour, baking powder, baking soda, and salt.

In a large bowl, whisk the eggs with the coconut oil, honey, almond milk, vanilla extract, and lemon juice until smooth.

Slowly transfer the flour mixture into the wet ingredients and whisk until completely smooth. Stir in lemon zest, and then pour mixture into loaf pan.

Cover the loaf with foil and bake for 35 minutes. Remove foil and bake for an additional 25 to 30 minutes or until a toothpick comes out clean when inserted in the middle.

Remove from the oven and allow to cool for 10 minutes.

In a medium bowl, combine the glaze ingredients and whisk until smooth. Using a spoon, drizzle the glaze over the top of the loaf.

Blueberry Oat Bread

The original recipe was published inside my first cookbook, *The Best Homemade Kids' Lunches on the Planet*. It's been my go-to bread loaf recipe for years. Of course, I had to recreate my original recipe for this book so the tradition could continue.

The results of testing this version were magical. A hearty oaty loaf with a crumbly and moist texture that made my house smell like a bowl of toasted oats with warm blueberries and earthy maple syrup! It's simply a delicious loaf of bread and I'm thrilled its legacy can continue on with this book. Your friends and family will love it; and soon, you'll find yourself making two loaves at once!

Yield: 1 loaf

2 cups (90 g) oat flour
2 teaspoons baking powder
½ teaspoon salt
½ cup (120 ml) honey or maple syrup
1 large banana, about 1 cup
½ cup (120 ml) melted coconut oil
2 eggs, at room temperature
1 teaspoon vanilla extract
2 teaspoons lemon zest
⅓ cup (33 g) old fashioned oats
1 cup (170 g) blueberries

Preheat the oven to 375°F (190°C). Line a 9 x 5-inch (23 x 10 cm) loaf pan with parchment paper.

In a large bowl, whisk together the oat flour, baking powder, and salt.

In a blender, place the honey or maple syrup, banana, coconut oil, eggs, vanilla extract, and lemon zest. Blend on medium speed until the ingredients are combined and you have a smooth, frothy texture.

Pour the wet mixture into the dry ingredient bowl, and slowly whisk until combined. Add in the oats, and mix, then gently fold the blueberries into the batter.

Pour the batter into the pan and bake 45 to 55 minutes or until a toothpick comes out clean. If your bread loaf is looking golden around minute 35, cover with foil.

Remove the loaf from the oven and allow it to cool down in the pan for 10 minutes before lifting the parchment paper out of the pan and slicing the blueberry loaf.

Chocolate Zucchini Bread

During a visit to our pediatrician, the doctor asked my son, "Which vegetables do you like eating?" To which he replied, "None, except zucchini in my mom's Chocolate Zucchini Bread. She thinks I don't know, but I saw her put it in there and I still eat it."

Moist, rich, and delicious, this is one recipe the kids won't notice is filled with veggies, unless you get sloppy like me and you get caught!

Yield: 1 loaf

---

1 ¾ cups (165 g) shredded zucchini, about 2 medium

1 ½ cups (170 g) oat flour

⅓ cup (40 g) unsweetened cocoa powder

1 teaspoon baking soda

¼ teaspoon salt

¼ cup (60 ml) melted coconut oil

¼ cup (62 g) almond butter

½ cup (95 g) coconut sugar

2 large eggs

1 teaspoon vanilla extract

½ cup (85 g) dark chocolate chips

For this recipe to be dairy-free, use allergy-friendly chocolate chips.

Place the shredded zucchini in a paper towel–lined colander and press down to remove any excess moisture.

Preheat your oven to 350°F (180°C) and line a 9 x 5-inch (23 cm x 13 cm) loaf pan with parchment paper.

In a medium bowl, combine the oat flour, cocoa powder, baking soda, and salt; set aside.

In a separate large bowl, combine the coconut oil, almond butter, coconut sugar, eggs, and vanilla extract until well combined and smooth.

Add the dry ingredients to the wet until just combined. Add in the shredded zucchini and chocolate chips, folding to combine.

Transfer batter to the prepared loaf pan and bake for 50 to 60 minutes or until a toothpick comes out clean when inserted in the center.

Remove from the oven and allow to cool for 10 minutes, before slicing and serving.

Refrigerate leftovers in an airtight container for up to 5 days.

Banana Oat Bread

How many times have you looked at the overly ripe bananas on your counter and thought to yourself, "I'll use those to make banana bread," and then, you don't. If you're anything like me, you decide to freeze them for a future smoothie, right?

Well, the beauty of this recipe is that you can make it with the bananas on your counter or the ones you saved for later in your freezer. It's a win-win!

Like the classic banana bread we all love, this version uses oat flour and honey to give it a light, moist texture.

Yield: 1 loaf

---

1 ½ cups (168 g) oat flour
1 ½ teaspoons baking soda
¼ teaspoon salt
½ cup (170 g) honey
1 teaspoon vanilla extract
¼ cup (60 ml) melted
   coconut oil
1 egg
1 cup (225 g) mashed bananas

Preheat the oven to 350°F (180°C). Line a loaf pan with parchment paper.

In a large bowl, combine the oat flour, baking soda, and salt. Stir to combine and set aside.

In a separate large bowl, combine the honey, vanilla extract, coconut oil, and egg; whisk to combine. Add the bananas and stir until smooth.

Working in batches, add the flour mixture to the wet ingredients and stir after each addition until a thick batter forms.

Pour the batter into the prepared loaf pan and bake for 50 minutes or until a toothpick comes out clean when inserted in the center.

Remove from the oven and allow to cool for 10 minutes before slicing.

Double Chocolate Banana Bread

When you secretly want cake but have "nothing to celebrate," you simply make this Double Chocolate Banana Bread recipe and keep the celebrating to yourself. I've been known to slather almond butter on a thick slice of this decadent treat and tell myself "you deserve a second." I can't help it. It's one of my favorite things to bake.

Yield: 1 loaf

---

3 medium bananas, ripened
2 eggs
1 tablespoon (16 g) almond butter
2 teaspoons (10 ml) vanilla extract
¾ cup (83 g) almond flour
⅓ cup (45 g) coconut flour
½ cup (59 g) unsweetened cocoa powder
½ teaspoon baking soda
¼ teaspoon salt
½ cup (85 g) dark chocolate chips

For this recipe to be dairy-free, use allergy-friendly chocolate chips.

Preheat oven to 350°F (180°C). Line an 8 x 4-inch (20 cm x 10 cm) loaf pan with parchment paper.

In a food processor or blender, combine the bananas, eggs, almond butter, and vanilla extract and process until smooth.

In a medium bowl, combine the almond flour, coconut flour, cocoa powder, baking soda, and salt and whisk together until well combined.

Add the wet ingredients to the dry ingredients and stir until well incorporated. Fold in the chocolate chips.

Pour the batter into the prepared loaf pan and bake for 25 minutes or until a toothpick comes out clean when inserted in the middle.

Remove from the oven and allow to cool 10 minutes before slicing and serving.

Pumpkin Spice Coffee Cake

When you can't decide between a pumpkin pie or cake, this is the dessert to make! Bonus points if you enjoy a slice with the Pumpkin Spice Latte (page 145).

Yield: 9 servings

Streusel Topping

⅔ cup (75 g) almond flour
⅓ cup (60 g) coconut sugar
¼ teaspoon salt
½ teaspoon pumpkin pie spice
⅓ cup (72 g) solid coconut oil

Coffee Cake

1 cup (118 g) almond flour
¼ cup (33 g) coconut flour
2 teaspoons (4 g) pumpkin pie spice
½ teaspoon baking soda
½ teaspoon salt
1 cup (245 g) pumpkin purée
¼ cup (85 g) honey or maple syrup
¼ cup (45 g) coconut sugar
¼ cup (60 ml) melted coconut oil
1 teaspoon vanilla extract
4 eggs

Preheat oven to 375°F (190°C) and grease a 9 x 9-inch (23 cm x 23 cm) square pan with coconut oil.

To make the streusel topping, in a medium bowl combine the almond flour, coconut sugar, salt, and pumpkin pie spice. Add the coconut oil and use a fork to stir it into the flour until a crumbly mixture begins to form.

Combine the almond and coconut flour, pumpkin pie spice, baking soda, and salt in a large bowl; set aside.

In a separate large bowl, combine the pumpkin purée, honey or maple syrup, coconut sugar, coconut oil, vanilla extract, and eggs. Whisk to form a smooth batter.

Add the dry ingredients to the wet and stir to combine until no lumps are visible. Set bowl aside for 5 minutes to allow coconut flour to absorb some of the moisture.

Pour half the batter in the prepared pan. Top it with half of the streusel mixture. Pour the remaining coffee cake batter into the pan and top with remaining streusel.

Bake for 30 to 40 minutes or until a toothpick comes out clean when inserted in the middle.

Remove from the oven and allow cake to cool for 10 minutes before slicing and serving.

By the Slice

BARS AND PIES

Lemon Bars

These lemon bars have a thick lemon filling over a sweet crust.
They're perfect for parties, family gatherings, and bake sales.

Yield: 12 servings

—

Crust
½ cup (120 ml) melted
  coconut oil
½ cup (95 g) coconut sugar
2 teaspoons (10 ml) vanilla
  extract
½ teaspoon salt
1 cup (113 g) oat flour

Filling
3 eggs plus 1 egg yolk
½ cup (120 ml) lemon juice,
  about 4 lemons
⅓ cup (115 g) honey
3 tablespoons (20 g) oat flour

Preheat the oven to 350°F (180°C). Line a square 9 x 9-inch (23 x 23 cm) baking pan with parchment paper.

In a large bowl, combine the melted coconut oil, coconut sugar, vanilla extract, and salt; whisk to combine. Add the oat flour and stir to completely combine. The dough will be thick.

Press the dough in an even layer into the baking pan and bake in the preheated oven for 16 to 18 minutes or until the edges are lightly browned.

While the crust bakes, add the eggs, egg yolk, lemon juice, and honey to a large bowl and whisk to combine. Add the oat flour and whisk until smooth.

Pour the filling over the warmed crust and bake the bars for 20 minutes or until the center is set.

Remove the bars from the oven and allow to cool down to room temperature before refrigerating for 2 hours or until chilled.

Once cooled, remove the bars from the oven and cut into 12 squares.

Refrigerate leftover bars in an airtight container for up to 1 week.

—

Kitchen Note

ⱱ *These bars freeze incredibly well once sliced and individually wrapped for up to a month.*

ⱱ *Shown: Powdered "confectioners' sugar" made from monk fruit is a clean option that is available at many retailers and online.*

Banana Chocolate Chip Bars

My friend Andrea took it upon herself to make "a few substitutions" while making my allergy-friendly banana bars on MOMables.com. I usually discourage this, especially among my friends, since I can't guarantee the outcome.

Little did we know that her ingenuity would yield these delicious bars! We've made these with fresh, ripe bananas and frozen bananas (thawed), and we are never disappointed.

Better yet, if you don't have bananas around, substitute the bananas for 1 cup (245 g) of canned pumpkin into the recipe and add ¾ teaspoon of cinnamon for a delicious variation that will fill your kitchen with incredible aromas.

Yield: 12 servings

———

2 bananas, mashed
2 eggs
½ cup (170 g) honey
¼ cup (60 ml) melted
   coconut oil
1 teaspoon vanilla extract
1 ½ cups (170 g) oat flour
½ teaspoon baking soda
¼ teaspoon salt
¾ cup (130 g) semi-sweet
   chocolate chips

———

For this recipe to be dairy-free, use allergy-friendly chocolate chips.

Preheat the oven to 350°F (180°C). Line a 9 x 9-inch (23 cm x 23 cm) square baking pan with parchment paper.

In a large bowl, combine the bananas, eggs, honey, coconut oil, and vanilla extract. Whisk until smooth.

In a separate medium bowl, combine the oat flour, baking soda, and salt.

Add the dry ingredients to the wet ingredients and mix until smooth.

Fold in the chocolate chips and pour the batter into the lined pan. Bake for 20 minutes or until golden brown.

Remove from the oven and allow to cool before slicing into 12 bars.

Blueberry Crumble Bars

I have a recipe on LauraFuentes.com for my auntie's blueberry pie and a recipe for blueberry coffee cake that are incredible. These crumble bars, however, have never made it to the blog because they are usually gone before I can photograph them, or I make them to share with friends.

For best results, use fresh blueberries since frozen ones add a lot of moisture to this recipe—you'll get a very moist (almost wet) bar that is not as nice to eat.

In case you are making these for yourself, know this: You can freeze them! Slice the bars, wrap, and freeze. Now you have enjoyment for weeks to come.

Yield: 9 bars

Crumble Layer
2 cups (236 g) almond flour
2 tablespoons (28 g) tapioca
  starch
¼ cup (60 ml) melted
  coconut oil
¼ cup (120 ml) maple syrup
1 teaspoon vanilla extract
¼ teaspoon salt

Blueberry Layer
3 cups (290 g) fresh blueberries
Juice of 1 lemon
3 tablespoons (45 ml) maple
  syrup
1 tablespoon (14 g) tapioca
  starch

Preheat the oven to 350°F (180°C). Line a 9 x 9-inch (23 cm x 23 cm) baking dish with parchment paper.

In a large bowl, combine the almond flour, tapioca starch, coconut oil, maple syrup, vanilla extract, and salt. Stir with a fork, until a thick, crumbly texture forms.

Push half of the mixture into the bottom of the prepared baking dish.

In a separate large bowl, combine the blueberries, lemon juice, maple syrup, and tapioca starch; stir to combine. Spread the blueberries in an even layer over the crumble layer.

Sprinkle the remaining half of the crumble layer over the blueberry layer.

Transfer to the oven and bake for 40 to 45 minutes or until the top begins to turn a golden brown.

Remove from oven and allow the bars to cool for 10 minutes before slicing and serving.

Raspberry Crumble Bars

Sweet, tart raspberries with a crumbled cookie-like topping—this is just the type of recipe that will impress your guests.

Yield: 12 servings

Base Layer
2 cups (290 g) raspberries
3 tablespoons (60 g) honey
2 tablespoons (30 ml) water
1 tablespoon (15 ml) fresh lemon juice
1 teaspoon vanilla extract
1 ½ tablespoons (11 g) chia seeds

Crumble Topping
½ cup (95 g) packed coconut sugar
1 cup (113 g) oat flour
¼ teaspoon baking soda
⅛ teaspoon salt
1 cup (80 g) old fashioned oats
½ cup (120 ml) melted coconut oil

Preheat oven to 350°F (180°C). Line a 9 x 9-inch (23 cm x 23 cm) square pan with parchment paper.

In a medium saucepan, combine the raspberries, honey, water, lemon juice, and vanilla extract. Stir to combine and bring to a full boil over medium heat.

Reduce the heat to low and simmer for 10 to 15 minutes or until the raspberries have softened. Mash mixture with a large fork or potato masher. Add the chia seeds and stir to combine. Allow the mixture to continue simmering for 8 to 10 minutes or until it has thickened.

Remove from heat and allow the raspberry mixture to cool down to room temperature.

Meanwhile, in a large bowl, combine the coconut sugar, oat flour, baking soda, salt, and old fashioned oats. Add the melted coconut oil and stir with a fork until the mixture is crumbly.

Press 2 cups of the mixture in the bottom of the prepared pan.

Spread the cooled raspberry mixture over the oat layer and sprinkle the remaining crumb mixture over the top, making sure to distribute it evenly throughout the pan.

Bake for 35 to 40 minutes or until the top is lightly browned.

Remove from oven and let it cool down to room temperature before slicing into bars.

Carrot Cake Bars

On MOMables.com, I have a Carrot Cake Bar recipe my family and thousands of internet visitors love. I knew I had to recreate a clean version to include in this cookbook when I made them last year for a group of friends.

These carrot cake bars have all the spices and texture of traditional carrot cake. I often make them without the frosting and just enjoy the cake.

Yield: 9 servings

—

½ cup (88 g) dates
¼ cup (60 ml) hot water
1 ½ cups (175 g) almond flour
1 teaspoon salt
½ teaspoon baking soda
1 teaspoon ground cinnamon
½ teaspoon ground nutmeg
3 large eggs
¼ cup (85 g) honey
2 tablespoons (30 ml) melted coconut oil
1 ½ cups (165 g) finely grated carrots
1 cup (120 g) coarsely chopped walnuts, plus additional for topping
Whipped Coconut Cream (page 17)

Preheat oven to 325°F (170°C). Line a 9 x 9-inch (23 cm x 23 cm) square pan with parchment paper.

Add the dates to the bowl of a food processor. Process until a thick paste forms, adding hot water as needed. Remove from the food processor and set aside.

In a large bowl, combine the almond flour, salt, baking soda, cinnamon, and nutmeg.

In a separate large bowl, combine the eggs, honey, and coconut oil; whisk until smooth.

Add the carrots and dates to the egg mixture, thoroughly folding to combine.

Working in batches, add the dry ingredients to the wet ingredients, stirring to incorporate the ingredients after each addition. Fold in the walnuts and pour the batter into the prepared cake pan.

Bake 40 minutes or until a toothpick comes out dry. Remove from the oven and allow to cool completely.

Spread the coconut whipped cream over the cooled cake and top with additional chopped walnuts.

—

Kitchen Note
♥ *These bars freeze great once sliced and individually wrapped.*

Pumpkin Pie

My mother loves pumpkin pie and asks me to make this recipe year-round. I'm giving you permission to not wait until the holiday season to make this classic dessert.

The pie "crust" in this recipe will never taste like raw dough, feel undercooked, or be left on a plate. You almost wish you had more of it, it's so good.

Yield: 8 servings

Crust

2 cups (136 g) almond flour
2 tablespoons (22 g) coconut
  sugar
¼ teaspoon salt
⅓ cup (72 g) solid coconut oil
1 egg, beaten

Filling

15-ounce (450 g) can pumpkin
  purée
2 eggs
¾ cup (180 g) coconut milk
⅓ cup (115 g) honey or maple
  syrup
¼ teaspoon salt
2 teaspoons (5 g) pumpkin pie
  spice

In a large bowl, combine the almond flour, coconut sugar, and salt. Add the coconut oil and, using a fork, combine the mixture until it resembles coarse sand. Add the egg and stir until a dough-like texture forms.

Form a ball and wrap it in plastic wrap. Refrigerate for an hour.

Preheat oven to 350°F (180°C).

Roll the dough into a 12-inch (30 cm) circle. Place the dough in a 9-inch (23 cm) pie dish. Place in the refrigerator until ready to fill.

In a large bowl, whisk the canned pumpkin, eggs, coconut milk, honey or maple syrup, salt, and pumpkin pie spice.

Remove the dough from the refrigerator and pour the filling into the pie dish.

Bake for 45 to 50 minutes or until the center of the pie is set.

Remove from the oven and allow to cool completely, for about 2 hours, before slicing and serving.

Chocolate Cream Pie

Now that you have this recipe, gone will be the days where you grab a chocolate pie from the grocery store. Let's get one thing straight: That's not real pie. It's chocolate pudding spread atop bland pastry crust.

This recipe, however, has a deliciously rich chocolate filling made with whipped coconut cream and cocoa powder that will give you that chocolate fix you need. And the crust? Hands down the best you'll ever have.

Yield: 8 servings

Crust
2 cups (236 g) almond flour
2 tablespoons (22 g) coconut
  sugar
¼ teaspoon salt
⅓ cup (72 g) solid coconut oil
1 egg, beaten

Filling
2 14-ounce (403 ml) cans
  coconut cream
⅓ cup (115 g) honey
⅔ cup (80 g) unsweetened
  cocoa powder
⅛ teaspoon salt
½ teaspoon vanilla extract

Whipped Coconut Cream
  (page 17), (optional), for
  serving

Preheat the oven to 350°F (180°C).

In a large bowl, combine the almond flour, coconut sugar, and salt. Add the coconut oil and use a fork to cut the oil into the almond flour, until the mixture resembles wet sand. Add the egg and stir to combine to form a dough.

Press the dough into a round disk, wrap with plastic wrap, and refrigerate for up to 1 hour.

On a lightly floured surface, roll the dough into a 12-inch (30 cm) circle, about ¼ to ½ inch thick. Lay it into a 9-inch (23 cm) pie dish. Bake the pie crust for 5 to 10 minutes or until golden brown on the edges and set. Remove from oven and allow to cool.

Scoop the white coconut cream out of the cans into a large bowl, discarding the remaining clear liquid at the bottoms of the cans.

Whisk the coconut cream until smooth. Add the honey, cocoa powder, salt, and vanilla extract and whisk to combine.

Pour the chocolate filling into the cooled pie crust and spread in an even layer.

Cover with plastic wrap and refrigerate for 2 hours or more.

To serve, remove it from the refrigerator, slice, and top with whipped coconut cream, if using.

No Crumbs Left!

COOKIES, SCONES, AND MORE

Soft Baked Gingersnaps

Like most of the cookies in this book, these gingersnaps are soft and chewy. The reason? We're a soft and chewy cookie family! The only time my kids complained about cookies is when we lived in Park City, Utah, for six weeks and no matter how early I'd take the cookies out of the oven, the high altitude and dry air would ruin it for them.

Our neighbors surprised us with a batch of these cookies and I've continued to make them ever since. For this book, I cleaned up the ingredients, and it is one my mother, who is a huge fan of gingersnap cookies, loves.

Yield: 12 cookies

¼ cup (62 g) almond butter
¼ cup (60 ml) melted
  coconut oil
¼ cup (45 g) coconut sugar
¼ cup (85 g) molasses
1 egg
1 teaspoon vanilla extract
1 cup (118 g) almond flour
⅓ cup (45 g) coconut flour
½ teaspoon baking soda
¼ teaspoon salt
1 teaspoon cinnamon
1 teaspoon ground ginger
¼ teaspoon allspice

Topping
2 tablespoons (22 g) coconut
  sugar
½ teaspoon cinnamon

Preheat oven to 350°F (180°C) and line a baking sheet with parchment paper.

In a large bowl, whisk the almond butter, coconut oil, coconut sugar, and molasses. Add in the egg and vanilla extract and whisk until the mixture is thoroughly combined.

In a medium bowl, sift the almond flour, coconut flour, baking soda, salt, cinnamon, ginger, and allspice.

Slowly, add the dry ingredients to the wet ingredients until a dough is formed. Cover and refrigerate for 30 minutes.

In a small bowl, combine coconut sugar and cinnamon.

Using a cookie scoop, scoop dough into your hands and roll into a ball. Roll each ball in the cinnamon sugar mixture.

Place each ball on the baking sheet and flatten with the back of a spoon. Bake for 8 to 10 minutes and remove from the oven while the cookies seem a little underdone. Allow them to cool before eating.

Chewy Snickerdoodles

Snickerdoodles are one of my husband's favorite cookies and this version has the perfect, chewy texture. With cinnamon and coconut sugar sprinkled over the top, the cookie practically melts in your mouth. You'll hear yourself go "hmmmm" as you bite into it.

Yield: 12 cookies

1 ¼ cups (146 g) almond flour
2 tablespoons (18 g) plus 1 teaspoon (5g) coconut flour
1 teaspoon baking powder
¼ teaspoon salt
¾ teaspoon cinnamon
⅓ cup (79 ml) melted coconut oil
⅓ cup (83 g) almond butter
¼ cup (85 g) maple syrup
¼ cup (45 g) coconut sugar
1 egg
1 teaspoon vanilla extract

Topping
3 tablespoons (33 g) coconut sugar
1 tablespoon (8 g) cinnamon

Preheat the oven to 350°F (180°C) and line a large baking sheet with parchment paper. Position the oven rack in the upper portion of oven.

In a medium bowl, combine the almond flour, coconut flour, baking powder, salt, and cinnamon; stir to combine.

In a separate large bowl, cream the coconut oil, almond butter, maple syrup, and sugar with a hand mixer on medium speed until smooth. Add the egg and vanilla extract, and mix on low speed until combined.

Slowly add the flour mixture to the wet ingredients and stir to combine, until a dough forms. Chill the dough for 20 to 30 minutes or until firm.

Use a cookie scoop or large spoon to scoop the dough into rounded tablespoonfuls and roll into balls.

In a small bowl, combine the coconut sugar and cinnamon. Roll each ball in the sugar mixture and place on the baking sheet. Use a large spoon to flatten each cookie.

Bake in the preheated oven for 11 to 13 minutes. Remove from the oven and allow cookies to cool down to room temperature before serving.

Flourless Chocolate Cookies

My original "flourless" chocolate chip cookie can be found inside my cookbook *The Best Grain-Free Meals on the Planet*. This recipe was supposed to make it into that book, but after many rounds of testing, I ran out of time to make baking magic and saved it for later.

This fudgy, cake-like cookie with crispy edges is one I'm happy to make when I want a simple, one-bowl recipe without flour.

Yield: 24 cookies

1 cup (250 g) almond butter
½ cup (95 g) coconut sugar
1 large egg
½ tablespoon (7 ml) vanilla
  extract
2 tablespoons (30 ml) water
⅓ cup (40 g) unsweetened
  cocoa powder
¼ cup (28 g) ground flax seeds
1 ½ teaspoons baking soda

Preheat oven to 350°F (180°C). Line 2 large baking sheets with parchment paper.

In a medium bowl, mix the almond butter, coconut sugar, egg, vanilla extract, and water until thoroughly combined.

Add the cocoa powder, flax seeds, and baking soda, and whisk until the cocoa powder is fully incorporated.

Transfer the dough to an airtight container and refrigerate for 1 hour. Use a cookie scoop or large spoon to scoop the dough into rounded tablespoonfuls onto the baking sheet.

Bake for 10 minutes or until the edges are set. The middles will be slightly soft. Allow the cookies to rest for 3 minutes before serving.

Kitchen Note
♥ *Refrigerate leftovers in an airtight container for up to 3 days.*

Oatmeal Raisin Cookies

Not including a clean version of the traditional oatmeal cookie inside this book would be a real tragedy for those who have an oatmeal cookie lover at home.

I know that for many of you the oatmeal raisin cookie wins over the traditional chocolate chip cookie because of its hearty texture. This recipe won't disappoint since it's got that perfect chewy texture and the cinnamon raisin combination everyone loves.

On a final note, you can omit the cinnamon and raisins and add about ½ cup (75 g) of chocolate chips and have the best of both worlds: the oatmeal chocolate chip!

Yield: 12 cookies

—

1 ½ cups (120 g) old fashioned oats, divided
1 cup (110 g) oat flour
½ teaspoon baking powder
½ teaspoon baking soda
1 teaspoon ground cinnamon
¼ teaspoon salt
⅓ cup (79 ml) melted coconut oil
¼ cup (45 g) coconut sugar
¼ cup (85 g) honey or maple syrup
2 eggs
1 teaspoon vanilla extract
¾ cup (90 g) raisins, packed

Preheat oven to 350°F (180°C). Line a baking sheet with parchment paper.

In a large bowl, combine the oats, oat flour, baking powder, baking soda, cinnamon, and salt. Whisk to combine.

In a separate large bowl, combine the coconut oil, coconut sugar, honey or maple syrup, eggs, and vanilla extract. Whisk until thoroughly combined.

Add the dry ingredients to the wet ingredients. Whisk until smooth. Fold in the raisins.

Using a medium cookie scoop, scoop cookie dough and drop onto the prepared baking sheet.

Using the back of a spoon, flatten cookies into rounds that are ½ inch (1.3 cm) thick.

Bake for 8 to 12 minutes or until golden brown. Remove from oven and allow to cool 5 minutes before serving.

—

Kitchen Note
♥ *Double or triple the recipe, scoop the dough onto a parchment-lined sheet pan, freeze, and transfer into a zip bag for future cookies!*

Lemon Macaroons

Originally shared in my cookbook *The Best Grain-Free Family Meals on the Planet*, this recipe has been recreated in a few different versions. A raspberry version, a minty version, a chocolate version, and my favorite: this lemon version.

I love macaroons. They remind me of special afternoon teatime with my grandmother during my childhood in Spain, because she loved to make these. While I was not a big fan of hot tea (I'm still not), I really loved these macaroons, and I've kept making them ever since.

Yield: 16 macaroons

2 large egg whites
¼ cup (85 g) honey
1 teaspoon vanilla extract
2 cups (190 g) unsweetened
  shredded coconut
Zest of 1 lemon

Preheat the oven to 250°F (120°C). Line a baking sheet with parchment paper.

In a large bowl, beat the egg whites with a hand mixer for 30 seconds, until foamy.

Add the honey and vanilla extract. Beat on high for 4 to 5 minutes or until stiff peaks form.

Gently fold in the coconut and lemon zest.

Scoop the batter by large spoonfuls onto the prepared sheet. Place the sheet in the preheated oven and bake for 25 to 27 minutes or until the tops are golden.

Remove from the oven and cool the macaroons to room temperature before transferring to a cooling rack to cool completely.

Baked Apple Crisp

Many weekends, I slice an apple on top of parchment paper, top it with cinnamon, finely chopped nuts, a little melted butter or coconut oil, some coconut flakes, a few oats, and toss everything around to combine before baking. This is what I call a "baked apple for breakfast" that feels like I'm indulging in apple pie.

Of course, I had to organize my "a little bit of this and a little bit of that" into a written recipe so this is what turned out after a little back and forth testing—not that I complained.

Yield: 8 servings

Apple Layer

6 medium Granny Smith, Pink Lady, or Honey Crisp apples, peeled and sliced to ¼-inch thickness
1 ½ teaspoons apple pie spice
1 tablespoon (15 ml) maple syrup

Crumble Topping

⅓ cup (79 ml) melted coconut oil
1 cup (125 g) walnuts
¾ cup (65 g) oat flour
2 tablespoons (30 ml) maple syrup
⅔ cup (60 g) unsweetened coconut flakes
1 teaspoon vanilla extract
2 ½ teaspoons (5 g) apple pie spice
⅛ teaspoon salt

Preheat your oven to 350°F (180°C). Grease a 9-inch (23 cm) pie dish or baking dish with coconut oil.

In a large bowl, toss the sliced apples with the apple pie spice and maple syrup. Transfer to the baking dish.

For the crumble topping, combine all the ingredients in a food processor and process or pulse until the walnuts are finely ground and the dough forms a thick, crumbly paste.

If your topping isn't thick, you can chill it for 5 to 10 minutes in the fridge. Spread the topping over the apples to completely cover.

Transfer to the oven and bake for 45 minutes or until the apples are bubbling and the topping is brown and crisp. If the top browns too soon, you can cover it with aluminum foil part of the way through.

Let sit for at least 30 minutes to cool down before serving warm.

Kitchen Note

♥ *Granny Smith, Pink Lady, or Honey Crisp apples will be the best choice for this recipe, as they have a sweet, tart taste and bake down beautifully in cobblers, pastries, and pies. Make sure to slice the apples into the same thickness to ensure that everything bakes evenly.*

Chocolate Chip Scones

Round, triangular, or drop scones—I don't care; I'll eat them all. While I'm known to enjoy one (or two) with coffee, I wanted to recreate one of my favorite treats into a cleaner version to share with you in this cookbook.

A true scone aficionado probably owns a scone pan, but I'm telling you that it's not needed as long as you can follow directions and let the oven do the rest.

Yield: 8 scones

---

1 ¾ cups (200 g) almond flour
⅓ cup (45 g) coconut flour
1 ½ teaspoon baking powder
½ teaspoons baking soda
¼ teaspoon salt
⅓ cup (60 g) coconut sugar
⅓ cup (72 g) solid coconut oil
⅓ cup (79 ml) almond milk
1 egg
2 teaspoons (10 ml) vanilla
  extract
½ cup (85 g) semi-sweet
  chocolate chips

For this recipe to be dairy-free, use allergy-friendly chocolate chips.

In a large bowl, combine the almond and coconut flour with the baking powder, baking soda, salt, and coconut sugar. Add the coconut oil and use a fork to cut it into the flour to form a crumbly texture. Set aside.

In a large bowl, combine the almond milk, egg, and vanilla extract; whisk until smooth.

Add the wet ingredients to the dry ingredients and stir into a smooth batter. Add the chocolate chips and fold to combine.

Place the dough in the freezer for 30 minutes.

Preheat the oven to 400°F (200°C).

Place the dough onto a sheet of parchment paper and knead lightly. Shape into a circle about 2 inches (5 cm) thick and cut into 8 triangles.

Lift and transfer the sheet of parchment paper onto a baking sheet. Bake for 17 to 20 minutes or until golden brown.

Remove from oven and allow to cool before serving.

Kitchen Notes

♥ *Omit the chocolate chips from the recipe and add up to ½ cup of dried fruit, nuts, or even fresh berries. Without the chocolate chips, you have a plain scone recipe you can use and modify to your liking!*

♥ *To make the coconut oil solid, place it in the refrigerator for 10 minutes before using.*

Lemon Blueberry Scones

Years ago, I wanted to see if I could recreate the blueberry scone from one of my favorite coffee shops into a cleaner, grain-free version. Originally published on LauraFuentes.com and later in *The Best Grain-Free Family Meals on the Planet*, this recipe was too good to not share it with my desserts-centric audience. I know that you are going to love this scone for breakfast, teatime, afternoon coffee, or snack.

For the round shape, I use a biscuit cutter. If you don't have one, use the rim of a tall glass.

Yield: 6 scones

1 ¾ cups (152 g) almond flour, sifted

3 tablespoons (27 g) coconut flour

¼ cup (85 g) honey

1 egg

¼ cup (60 ml) almond milk, divided

3 tablespoons (45 ml) melted coconut oil

1 teaspoon lemon zest

½ teaspoon baking soda

¼ teaspoon salt

½ cup (73 g) fresh blueberries

Preheat the oven to 350°F (180°C).

Sift your almond and coconut flours directly into a stand mixer. Add honey, egg, 3 tablespoons (45 ml) almond milk, coconut oil, lemon zest, baking soda, and salt to the flours. Mix until a loose dough forms. Gently fold in blueberries.

Using your biscuit cutter as a shaper, fill it with ½ to ¾ inch of dough. Press it down with your hands to form a scone over a lined baking sheet and lift the cutter as you hold down the dough to release. Repeat with remaining dough.

Brush scones with remaining 1 tablespoon (15 ml) almond milk.

Bake for 18 to 20 minutes or until golden brown. Allow them to cool down slightly prior to eating.

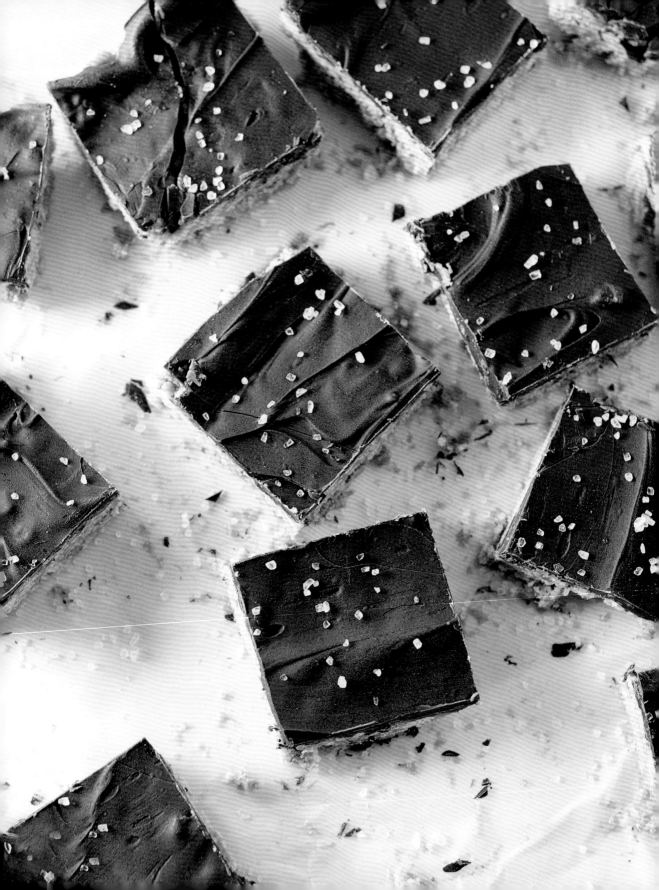

CHAPTER THREE

No-Bake Treats

Everyone needs an arsenal of no-bake recipes in their back pocket for times when the oven is out of commission, the AC is working overtime, or you simply want to mix, shape, and set it for later.

Many of the recipes in this chapter are perfectly portioned, because sometimes all you need are a couple of bites to satisfy your cravings.

From fun-to-eat, bite-sized treats, delightful bars to eat with friends, and wonderful pies and cheesecakes to serve at any occasion, these will be among the most used recipes in this book.

—

Bite-Sized and Delish

Matcha Green Tea Bites

If you enjoy matcha green tea, you're going to love this portable, full of nutrition, bite-size option!

Yield: 8 to 10 bites

2 cups (190 g) unsweetened shredded coconut
⅓ cup (37 g) almond flour
3 tablespoons (60 g) honey or maple syrup
1 tablespoon (15 ml) melted coconut oil
1 tablespoon (6 g) matcha green tea powder

Combine all ingredients in a food processor, cover, and process until a thick dough is formed.

Using a large spoon or small cookie scoop, scoop the dough and shape into 1-inch balls.

Refrigerate for 1 hour or until firm.

Kitchen Note

♥ *Refrigerate extra energy bites in an airtight container for up to 2 weeks.*

Orange Coconut Snack Bites

These coconut bites are an easy treat to whip up and will keep you satiated for a few hours thanks to the healthy fats from the shredded coconut and coconut oil.

Yield: 30 bites

———

3 cups (285 g) unsweetened
   shredded coconut
1 orange rind, zested
2 teaspoons (10 ml) fresh
   orange juice
⅓ cup (70 ml) melted
   coconut oil
⅔ cup (227 g) honey

Line a large baking sheet with parchment paper.

In a large mixing bowl, combine all the ingredients and stir until smooth.

Scoop the mixture into rounded tablespoonfuls and, using your hands, roll into balls.

Place the bites onto the prepared baking sheet and refrigerate for up to 1 hour or until firm.

———

Kitchen Note

♥ *Swap the orange with another citrus flavor like lemon or 2 teaspoons of lime zest. Refrigerate leftovers in an airtight container for up to a week.*

Pecan Pie Bites

Inspired by a favorite holiday pie, these bites are a healthier
fix for your sweet tooth and much easier to make.

Yield: 16 bites

———

1 cup (155 g) raisins or dates
1 cup (110 g) pecans
¼ cup (25 g) unsweetened
  shredded coconut
1 teaspoon vanilla extract
1 teaspoon cinnamon
¼ teaspoon nutmeg
¼ teaspoon ground ginger
⅛ teaspoon salt

In a medium bowl, soak the raisins in hot water for 10 minutes,
and drain.

In a food processor, combine the raisins or dates and pecans;
pulse to form a smooth paste. Add coconut, vanilla extract,
cinnamon, nutmeg, ginger, and salt.

Pulse a few times until combined. Refrigerate for 30 minutes
or until firm.

Using a cookie scoop or spoon, scoop and form the dough
into 16 small balls.

———

Kitchen Note
ᴠ *Refrigerate leftovers in an airtight container for up to a week.*

Carrot Cake Bites

You already know how I feel about carrot cake, right? It's the one cake I'd take with me to a deserted island to celebrate my birthday—or any occasion—for the rest of my life. But not all days are meant to be celebrated equally, and these bite-size treats make my everyday snacking feel special.

These are easy to assemble, with the food processor doing most of the work. If you don't have dates on hand, swap them for golden or regular raisins.

Yield: 20 bites

———

1 cup (175 g) dates
½ cup (60 g) walnuts
½ cup (56 g) pecans
¾ cup (60 g) oats
½ teaspoon cinnamon
¼ teaspoon nutmeg
¼ teaspoon salt
1 teaspoon vanilla extract
1 cup (110 g) shredded carrots
Unsweetened coconut for
 rolling

In a medium saucepan, bring 1 to 2 cups (235 ml to 475 ml) water to a boil. Remove from heat and add the dates, allowing them to soak for 20 minutes. Drain excess water.

Meanwhile, in a food processor, combine the walnuts, pecans, oats, cinnamon, nutmeg, salt, and vanilla extract. Process on medium speed until finely ground.

Add the soaked dates and shredded carrots and process until well combined. If the mixture is sticky, add ¼ cup (20 g) to ⅓ cup (35 g) of additional oats. If it seems too dry, add more water, 1 tablespoon at a time, until you reach the desired consistency.

Using a cookie scoop, scoop and shape the mixture into 20 balls.

Place the coconut in a shallow dish and roll each bite to coat.

———

Kitchen Note

𝓋 *Store the bites in an airtight container and refrigerate for up to 1 week.*

Chocolate Truffles

These are the type of truffles that will make any chocolate lover feel like they should find a chocoholics support group. Rich and decadent, they taste and feel like the ones sold at confectionary chocolate shops.

The dates provide the sweetness and almond butter gives them a fudgy texture. The end result is a perfectly sweet and smooth chocolate treat.

Yield: 15 truffles

12 pitted dates
½ cup (57 g) almond flour
⅔ cup (166 g) almond butter
3 tablespoons (21 g) unsweetened cocoa powder
¼ teaspoon salt
Finely chopped almonds (optional), for rolling
Cocoa powder (optional), for rolling

Add the dates to a medium bowl and cover with hot water. Soak for 10 minutes or until softened; drain.

In a high-speed blender, blend the dates until smooth, scraping down the sides of the blender as necessary. Add the almond flour, almond butter, cocoa powder, and salt.

Blend until completely smooth, scraping down the sides as necessary.

Use a small cookie scoop or a tablespoon to make rounded tablespoonfuls. Use your hands to roll into balls.

Place the chopped almonds and cocoa powder in separate, shallow bowls, if using. Roll each truffle in the almonds or cocoa powder.

Kitchen Note

ⓥ *Store in an airtight container in the refrigerator for up to a week.*

Lemon Blueberry Bites

With this recipe, every day can be a lemon blueberry muffin day. Except you can enjoy these snack bites on the go at any time of the day. While muffins are great, they require baking and, with three kids, I don't always have time for that!

This recipe is easy, so my kids can make it start to finish.

GF **DF** **EF** **V**

Yield: 24 bites

———

1 cup (95 g) sliced almonds
Zest and juice of 1 lemon
¼ cup (85 g) honey
1 ¼ cups (100 g) quick-cooking oats
½ cup (60 g) dried blueberries

In a food processor, process almonds, lemon zest, lemon juice, and honey until smooth.

Add half the oats and process until smooth.

Move mixture to a bowl and stir in remaining oats and blueberries. Stir until combined.

Using a large spoon, scoop the dough and shape into 1-inch balls.

Refrigerate leftovers in an airtight container for up to 2 weeks.

———

Kitchen Notes

♥ *Make sure to use dried blueberries because fresh or frozen will squish and create too much liquid while you're trying to form the snack bites.*

♥ *Swap the dried blueberries for dried cranberries and the lemon for orange zest for a delicious fall-themed snack.*

Oatmeal Raisin Bites

This recipe was one of the first ones I published on MOMables.com many moons ago because they're perfect to toss inside a lunchbox or enjoy as an afternoon snack.

Yield: 18 to 20 bites

———

1 cup (80 g) quick oats
1 cup (95 g) unsweetened
  shredded coconut
½ cup (56 g) ground flax seed
½ cup (85 g) mini chocolate
  chips (optional)
½ cup (78 g) raisins
½ cup (125 g) almond butter or
  peanut butter
⅓ cup (115 g) honey
1 teaspoon vanilla extract

———

For this recipe to be dairy-free, use allergy-friendly chocolate chips.

In a large bowl, combine the oats, coconut, flax seed, mini chocolate chips, if using, and raisins.

In a small bowl, whisk together the almond butter or peanut butter, honey, and vanilla extract.

Pour the almond butter or peanut butter mixture into the oat mixture and stir to thoroughly combine. Cover and allow to chill in the refrigerator for half an hour.

Once it is chilled, use a cookie scoop or spoon to scoop the mixture and roll into balls. Store in an airtight container and keep refrigerated for up to 1 week.

Peanut Butter No-Bake Cookies

Chewy, soft peanut butter cookies that require no baking—they're perfect for a mid-summer snack when turning on the oven will kill all the efforts from your AC.

Yield: 12 cookies

¾ cup (185 g) natural peanut butter
½ cup (170 g) honey
1 teaspoon vanilla extract
3 cups (340 g) oat flour
½ teaspoon salt

Line a large baking sheet with parchment paper.

In a microwave-safe bowl, combine the peanut butter and honey. Microwave in 30-second increments, stirring after each interval, until melted. Stir in the vanilla extract.

Add the oat flour and salt; stir to combine.

Using a cookie scoop, scoop the dough into your hands and roll into balls.

Place a ball onto the baking sheet and press down with the back of a fork to form a crisscross pattern. Repeat with remaining dough.

Place the baking sheet of cookies in the fridge for 10 to 20 minutes or until firm. Remove and enjoy.

Almond Butter Cups

I'm *that mom* who steals her kids' peanut butter cups from their Halloween stash. I usually hide them in a zip bag, behind the frozen fruit, in the garage freezer. It's a really sad moment when they are gone. And once they are gone, I make these.

These are even better, in my opinion, and hard to resist. The coconut flour is what gives the almond butter that thicker texture I love from the store-bought kind.

You can use a mini muffin pan or regular 12-count muffin tin. Store your stash in the freezer; otherwise they become soft and melty . . . and we don't want that.

Yield: 12 or 24 cups, depending on the pan used

½ cup (125 g) unsalted, creamy almond butter
1 tablespoon (20 g) honey or maple syrup
1 tablespoon (9 g) coconut flour
2 cups (350 g) dark chocolate chips
1 tablespoon (15 ml) melted coconut oil

Kitchen Note

♥ *To store, freeze leftover almond cups in an airtight container for 1 to 2 months.*

For this recipe to be dairy-free, use allergy-friendly chocolate chips.

Line a standard 12-cup muffin pan or a 24–mini muffin pan with paper liners. Set aside.

In a small bowl, combine the almond butter, honey or maple syrup, and coconut flour; whisk until smooth. Cover with plastic wrap and place in the freezer for 15 to 20 minutes, allowing the filling to chill and harden for easier molding.

Remove the bowl from the freezer. Scoop 2 teaspoons of filling into your hands and mold into a flat ¼-inch disk. Place the disk into a muffin cup. Repeat with remaining dough.

In a medium, microwave-safe bowl, combine chocolate and coconut oil. Microwave in 30-second increments, stirring after each interval until the chocolate is melted. Whisk until smooth.

Drop 2 teaspoons of melted chocolate into each muffin cup. Tap the pan to smooth chocolate into an even layer. Place an almond butter disk on top of the chocolate and top with 2 more teaspoons of melted chocolate. Repeat with remaining ingredients.

Place muffin pan into freezer for 15 to 20 minutes. Remove from the freezer and thaw for 10 to 20 minutes before serving.

Bars and By-the-Spoonful

Cherry Almond Granola Bars

I once purchased dried cherries in bulk thinking they were dried cranberries. They sat in my pantry for a few months until I realized that they could be used in my almond granola bars.

These granola bars are the perfect go-to treat for active days when you need something to satisfy that sweet tooth without straying from your goals. The cherry and almond combo sets them apart, but if you don't have dried cherries on hand, swap them for dried cranberries or blueberries.

GF **DF** **EF**

Yield: 12 bars

———

2 cups (160 g) old fashioned oats
1 ½ cups (40 g) brown rice cereal
¼ cup (24 g) unsweetened shredded coconut
¼ cup (30 g) chopped almonds
¼ teaspoon salt
½ cup (125 g) almond butter
½ cup (170 g) honey
1 teaspoon vanilla extract
¾ cup (90 g) dried cherries

Line a 9 x 13-inch (22 cm x 33 cm) pan with parchment paper.

In a large bowl, combine the oats, cereal, coconut, almonds, and salt.

In a microwave-safe bowl, combine the almond butter, honey, and vanilla extract. Microwave for 30 seconds or until the mixture is melted.

Pour the honey mixture into the oat mixture and stir to combine. Add the cherries and fold to mix.

Transfer the granola mixture into the prepared pan and press down in an even layer. Cover with plastic wrap and place in the refrigerator until solid, for about 1 hour.

Remove bars from refrigerator and cut into 12 squares.

———

Kitchen Note
♡ *Store leftovers in an airtight container for a week.*

Chunky Everything Granola Bars

My husband: "What are you doing?"

Me: "Making granola bars."

Husband: "So basically, dump the contents of the pantry and you turn them into granola bars?"

Me: "Pretty much!"

Pecans, almonds, cashews, raisins, and chocolate—these granola bars have it all!

Yield: 16 bars

1 cup (110 g) pecan halves
1 cup (110 g) almonds
1 cup (140 g) cashews
1 cup (95 g) unsweetened
  shredded coconut
1 teaspoon cinnamon
1 cup (155 g) raisins
½ teaspoon salt
¼ cup (60 ml) melted
  coconut oil
¼ cup (62 g) almond butter
⅓ cup (115 g) honey
1 teaspoon vanilla extract
½ cup (85 g) dark chocolate
  chips

For this recipe to be dairy-free, use allergy-friendly chocolate chips.

Line a 9 x 9-inch (23 cm x 23 cm) pan with parchment paper.

Combine the pecans, almonds, and cashews in a food processor. Cover with lid and pulse to chop the ingredients; don't overmix.

Transfer the nut mixture to a large mixing bowl and stir in the coconut, cinnamon, raisins, and salt.

In a small saucepan, combine the melted coconut oil, almond butter, and honey over medium-low heat. Whisk until smooth, and stir in the vanilla extract.

Add the coconut oil mixture to the dry ingredients and stir to fully combine. Once combined, fold in the chocolate chips.

Transfer the mixture to the prepared pan and press down in an even layer. Cover with plastic wrap and refrigerate for 1 hour or until firm.

Remove the bars from the refrigerator, remove from the pan, and cut into 16 bars to serve.

Kitchen Note

♥ *Bars will start to melt around room temperature due to the coconut oil, so they'll need to be kept chilled to stay firm.*

♥ *Store leftovers in the refrigerator in an airtight container for up to 2 weeks or freeze for up to 2 months.*

Chocolate Almond Butter Bars

You know how I feel about the Almond Butter Cups on page 86, but sometimes this girl wants more of the almond butter middle than those bite-sized treats provide. This bar is like flipping the recipe and eating more of the middle and less chocolate.

Every bite is like biting into a sweet and salty treat. Make sure to not skimp on the coarse sea salt because these will have you going to the moon and back!

Yield: 16 bars

———

1 cup (250 g) plus 2 tablespoons (32 g) creamy almond butter
¼ cup (85 g) honey
½ cup (67 g) coconut flour
4 ounces (175 g) dark chocolate, finely chopped
Coarse sea salt, for topping

———

For this recipe to be dairy-free, use allergy-friendly chocolate.

Line a 9 x 9-inch (23 cm x 23 cm) pan with parchment paper; set aside.

In a large bowl, combine the 1 cup of almond butter, honey, and coconut flour. Press the mixture into the pan and refrigerate for 30 minutes or until set.

In a medium microwave-safe bowl, combine the dark chocolate and the remaining 2 tablespoons of almond butter. Microwave in 30-second increments, stirring between each, until the chocolate is melted and smooth.

Pour the chocolate over the almond butter base and spread to cover the top. Cover with plastic wrap and refrigerate for 2 hours or until set.

Remove from the fridge and cut into 16 bars.

———

Kitchen Note

♥ *Keep these bars refrigerated or in the freezer, in an airtight container, for up to 2 weeks.*

Moon Bars

Like the Empress's castle in the movie *The Neverending Story*, you'll find pieces disappearing, one by one. The Empress, Moon Child, didn't get her name until the very end of the movie, where Bastian shouts out her name in a desperate attempt to save her.

For months, I found myself coming back to the freezer, breaking off one small piece, savoring it, and racking my brain for a name that would properly fit the recipe. The day before I turned in the final manuscript for this cookbook, I jokingly named them Moon "Child" Bars.

These bars aren't just great; they are epic. And like all good stories, you don't want them to end.

Yield: 12 bars

——

Bottom Layer
½ cup (55 g) almonds
½ cup (55 g) pecan halves
2 pitted dates

Middle Layers
1 cup (250 g) melted coconut
   butter
1 ¼ cups (220 g) pitted dates
¼ cup (60 ml) hot water

Top Layer
½ cup (85 g) dark chocolate
   chips
1 tablespoon (15 ml) coconut oil
Coarse sea salt

——

For this recipe to be dairy-free, use allergy-friendly chocolate chips.

To the bowl of a food processor, add the almonds, pecans, and dates. Cover and process until a thick dough forms. Firmly press the crust into a lined 9 x 9-inch (23 cm x 23 cm) baking dish.

Melt the coconut butter and pour over the crust. Freeze for 1 hour or until firm.

Add the dates and hot water to the food processor and process until a thick paste forms. Spread date mixture over the frozen bars and set aside in the freezer.

In a microwave-safe dish, combine the chocolate and coconut oil. Microwave in 30-second increments until melted, stirring with a fork until smooth.

Pour the chocolate over the bars and spread in an even layer. Sprinkle coarse sea salt over the top. Freeze until set, about 2 hours.

To serve, remove from freezer and allow to thaw for 10 minutes before slicing into 12 bars.

——

Kitchen Note
♡ *Store in an airtight container in the refrigerator for up to a week or freeze for up to a month.*

Chocolate Chip Blondies

With millions of pageviews, this recipe for Chocolate Chip Blondies is one of the most popular recipes on LauraFuentes.com. It's the type of treat you can feel good about eating, and the fact that they are no-bake eliminates a lot of mess!

I had been trying to create an edible cookie dough with no success. One day, I refrigerated this dough thinking "I'll come back to it later," and when I took the mixture out of the fridge it was in a solid state I could press down onto a pan, slice, and take with me.

Sometimes, I roll the dough into bite-sized balls and pack them inside my office lunch and my kids' lunches. They are one irresistible treat I know you're going to love.

GF   DF   EF

Yield: 6 squares

½ cup (150 g) mashed banana
¼ cup (62 g) peanut butter
¼ cup (85 g) honey or maple
  syrup
½ teaspoon vanilla extract
½ cup (67 g) plus 2 tablespoons
  (14 g) coconut flour, sifted
2 tablespoons (20 g) mini
  chocolate chips

For this recipe to be dairy-free, use allergy-friendly chocolate chips.

Line an 8 x 4-inch (20 cm x 10 cm) loaf pan with parchment paper.

In a large bowl, combine the mashed banana with the peanut butter, honey or maple syrup, and vanilla extract. Once the mixture is smooth, add the coconut flour and combine to form a thick dough.

Add the chocolate chips and fold to combine.

Spread mixture into a lined pan with your hands, pressing down and spreading evenly, to about ½-inch (1 cm) thickness. Refrigerate for 1 to 2 hours or until firm.

Picking up the parchment paper, remove from pan and cut into individual squares.

Store leftovers in an airtight container and refrigerate them for a week.

Kitchen Note

♡ *Make sure to measure the mashed banana, because coconut flour is not a very forgiving ingredient. You can add up to ¼ cup (25 g) vanilla protein powder for an extra protein boost.*

Chocolate Chip Cookie Dough Bars

These cookie dough bars were one of the failed attempts at making blondies. I was told by "someone" that blondies should not have nuts or dates.

I didn't want to scratch the recipe completely, so I saved it for later. One day, while walking the aisles of Target, I grabbed a few date bars by a popular brand for an upcoming trip. A few days later, while walking around New York, I opened one of those bars and I immediately thought "These taste like my failed bars!"

When I came home, I made them once more, photographed them, and shared the recipe on my website under this name since they truly taste like the store-bought bars. The best part is that they are much more cost-effective to make.

GF **DF** **EF** **V**

Yield: 12 bars

___

2 cups (280 g) raw cashew
  pieces
12 pitted dates
½ teaspoon vanilla extract
¼ teaspoon salt
¼ cup (42 g) mini chocolate
  chips or chocolate chunks

___

Substitute pumpkin seeds (pepitas) or sunflower seeds for the cashews for a nut-free recipe.

For this recipe to be dairy-free, use allergy-friendly chocolate chips.

Line a 9 x 9-inch (23 cm x 23 cm) pan with parchment paper.

In the bowl of a food processor, pulse the cashew pieces and dates until they begin to form a paste. Add in the vanilla extract and salt, and process until a paste forms. Add in chocolate chips and pulse to combine.

Transfer the mixture to the bottom of the pan and press down in an even layer. Refrigerate for 1 to 2 hours or until firm.

Pick up the parchment paper to remove the contents, and cut into individual bars. Wrap individually with plastic wrap and store in the refrigerator for up to 1 week.

Salted Peanut Butter Treats

This is the grown-up version of the favorite kid treat. When I made these for the first time, giggling more than my eight-year-old would, my best friend said, "Well, that's adulting for you!"

These salty peanut butter squares are everything you love about Rice Krispies treats but with peanut butter and chocolate! These have that crispy rice cereal layer with a thick, dark chocolate topping. Go ahead and double the recipe; you'll want the extra!

Yield: 12 squares

———

¾ cup (186 g) natural peanut butter
⅓ cup (115 g) honey
2 tablespoons (30 ml) melted coconut oil
1 teaspoon vanilla extract
¼ teaspoon salt
3 cups (75 g) crispy brown rice cereal

Chocolate Topping
1 cup (175 g) dark chocolate chips
Coarse sea salt, for sprinkling

———

For this recipe to be dairy-free, use allergy-friendly chocolate chips.

Line a 9 x 9-inch (23 cm x 23 cm) pan with parchment paper. Set aside.

In a medium saucepan, combine the peanut butter, honey, coconut oil, vanilla extract, and salt over medium heat. Stir until smooth, about 1 minute.

Add the crispy brown rice cereal and stir until combined and the cereal is completely coated. Pour into prepared pan and press down in an even layer.

Add the chocolate to a microwave-safe bowl. Microwave on high in 30-second increments, stirring after each interval, until chocolate is completely melted.

Pour the melted chocolate over the bars and spread in an even layer. Refrigerate for 30 minutes or until bars are completely cool and chocolate is solid. Sprinkle with fancy sea salt and slice into 12 squares.

———

Kitchen Note
♡ *Refrigerate leftovers in an airtight container for up to a week.*

Homemade Chunky Bars

If you like the classic chocolate bar, then you'll fall in love with this homemade version. Originally shared on LauraFuentes.com many years back, it's a recipe I keep coming back to time and time again, so I found it worthy of sharing with you.

Over the years, I've made large batches of this recipe, spreading it inside a baking pan, crumbling it, and bagging it inside cellophane bags as holiday gifts. The sweet and salty combination is one that's always a hit.

Yield: 12 bars

———

2 cups (350 g) dark chocolate chips
⅓ to ½ cup (52 g to 78 g) raisins
⅓ to ½ cup (40 g to 60 g) peanuts, coarsely chopped

———

For this recipe to be dairy-free, use allergy-friendly chocolate chips.

Line an 8 x 4-inch (20 cm x 10 cm) loaf pan with parchment paper and set aside.

In a double boiler, melt the chocolate chips over medium-low heat.

Evenly distribute the raisins and peanuts in the base of the pan.

Once the chocolate is melted, carefully pour it over the raisins and nuts, spread it in a smooth layer, and allow to cool down to room temperature before refrigerating the chocolate for 4 hours or until firm.

When ready to eat, remove from the refrigerator and cut into 12 bars.

Salted Tahini Cookie Dough Fudge

I always keep a jar of tahini to make my dad's famous hummus and salad dressing in the fridge. Last year, when my parents moved to another state and needed to empty out their fridge, they brought over all of the contents. Needless to say, I was "gifted" four jars of tahini.

"How much hummus can one consume?" I thought to myself. So, the quest began to find new uses for this popular ingredient. My dad suggested using it in desserts and, together, we created this fudge-like treat.

Tahini, when combined with honey, becomes sweet. The nutty seed's richness is what sets this fudge apart.

Yield: 16 fudge squares

—

1 cup (250 g) tahini
¼ cup (60 ml) melted
   coconut oil
2 tablespoons (40 g) honey or
   maple syrup
½ tablespoon vanilla extract
¼ teaspoon salt
⅓ cup (60 g) mini dark
   chocolate chips, divided
Coarse sea salt, for sprinkling

—

For this recipe to be dairy-free, use allergy-friendly chocolate chips.

Line an 8 x 4-inch (20 cm x 10 cm) loaf pan with parchment paper.

In a medium bowl, combine the tahini, coconut oil, honey or maple syrup, vanilla extract, and salt until smooth. Fold in ¼ cup (42 g) chocolate chips and pour the mixture into the prepared pan.

Refrigerate for 30 minutes. Remove from the refrigerator and sprinkle the remaining chocolate chips over the fudge and press down to set into the fudge.

Refrigerate until firm, about 1 to 2 hours.

Once set, sprinkle with coarse sea salt and slice through the middle and across into 16 squares.

—

Kitchen Note
♥ *Freeze leftover fudge in an airtight container for up to 3 months.*

Magic Bars

The crunchy peanut butter base and caramel-like top layer take these bars over the top. A word of caution: You might find yourself with a fork on hand, at 3 a.m., stealing another bite from the fridge. No, that's never happened to me before . . .

Yield: 12 bars

—

Bottom Layer
1 ½ cups (175 g) almond flour
½ cup (125 g) crunchy or smooth peanut butter
2 tablespoons (30 ml) melted coconut oil
⅓ cup (115 g) honey or maple syrup
¾ cup (72 g) unsweetened shredded coconut

Top Layer
1 tablespoon (15 ml) melted coconut oil
¾ cup (130 g) pitted dates, coarsely chopped
¼ cup (60 ml) hot water
1 tablespoon (20 g) honey or maple syrup
¼ teaspoon salt
3 tablespoons (30 g) dark chocolate chips
3 tablespoons (18 g) unsweetened shredded coconut

Line a 9 x 5-inch (23 cm x 13 cm) loaf pan with parchment paper.

In the bowl of a food processor, combine the ingredients for the peanut butter crust (Bottom Layer). Process for 1 to 2 minutes or until mixture begins to hold together and form a ball.

Transfer the peanut butter crust into the prepared pan and press down. Cover and refrigerate while preparing the top layer.

For the top layer, place the coconut oil, dates, water, honey or maple syrup, and salt into the bowl of a food processor. Process for 2 minutes or until completely smooth, stopping every 20 to 30 seconds to scrape the sides.

Spread the caramel glaze over the peanut butter crust.

Sprinkle the chocolate chips and coconut over the glaze. Cover and refrigerate for at least 1 hour or until firm.

Cut into 12 bars and serve. Store the bars in an airtight container for up to 2 weeks.

—

For this recipe to be dairy-free, use allergy-friendly chocolate chips.

Strawberry Shortcake Bars

These bars are an ode to the super popular Southern dessert, strawberry shortcake. Instead of sponge cake, sliced strawberries, and whipped topping, this recipe uses a grain-free pecan crust with creamy, fruity topping for a blissful, chilled dessert that's perfect for summer.

Yield: 9 bars

—

Crust

1 cup (110 g) pecans

1 cup (175 g) pitted dates, soaked

2 tablespoons (30 ml) melted coconut oil

¼ teaspoon salt

Filling

2 cups (280 g) soaked cashews

½ cup (118 ml) coconut cream

⅓ cup (115 g) honey

2 tablespoons (30 ml) melted coconut oil

1 teaspoon vanilla extract

1 tablespoon (15 ml) lemon juice

1 cup (145 g) sliced strawberries

Line a 9 x 9-inch (23 cm x 23 cm) square pan with parchment paper and grease the sides with coconut oil. Set aside.

Add the dates to a medium bowl and cover with hot water. Soak for 10 minutes until softened; drain.

Add the pecans, dates, coconut oil, and salt to a food processor. Process on medium speed until a sticky dough forms.

Spread the base dough into the prepared pan and press down into an even layer. Place in the freezer to set.

For the cheesecake mixture, add all of the filling ingredients to a high-speed blender and blend until smooth.

Remove the crust from the freezer and pour the cheesecake filling into the crust. Cover and place in the freezer to set for 4 hours or overnight.

Remove cheesecake from freezer and allow to thaw at room temperature for 10 to 15 minutes before serving. Slice into 9 bars and serve.

—

Kitchen Note

♥ *Refrigerate in an airtight container for up to a week.*

Chocolate Fudge

What was meant to be a no-bake brownies recipe turned into a decadent chocolate fudge. It reminds me of the fudge you buy by the slice at a popular mountain fudge shop but with cleaner ingredients.

Unlike its counterpart, this version tends to soften when left out at room temperature, so make sure to keep these refrigerated until you need them. Better yet, freeze them and pull them out when you need a quick chocolatey pick-me-up!

Yield: 12 squares

—

½ cup (125 g) almond butter

½ cup (120 ml) melted coconut oil

3 tablespoons (60 g) honey or maple syrup

¾ cup (90 g) unsweetened cocoa powder

⅛ teaspoon salt

2 ½ tablespoons (13 g) coconut flour

¼ cup (30 g) raw walnuts, roughly chopped

Chocolate Icing

¼ cup (45 g) chocolate chips

¼ teaspoon coconut oil

—

For this recipe to be dairy-free, use allergy-friendly chocolate chips.

Line a 9 x 9-inch (23 cm x 23 cm) square pan with parchment paper.

Place almond butter, coconut oil, honey or maple syrup, cocoa powder, and salt in the bowl of a food processor. Process until just blended, stopping to scrape down sides as needed.

Add the coconut flour and process until a ball of dough starts to form.

Transfer dough to a clean bowl. Add the walnuts and fold to combine. Press the mixture into the lined baking pan and refrigerate.

In a microwave-safe dish, combine the chocolate chips and coconut oil. Microwave in 30-second increments, stirring after each interval, until smooth.

Drizzle the fudge with the chocolate icing and refrigerate for 1 hour or until firm.

Remove from the fridge, cut into 12 squares, and serve.

Chocolate Hazelnut Spread

Growing up in Spain, I had my share of Nutella sandwiched between two Maria cookies. It was an afternoon treat I would enjoy with a glass of milk or some fruit.

My youngest son is a huge fan of the Nutella spread and, if left unattended, he will eat this version by the spoonful! It has a smooth texture that's perfect for spreading onto fruit, toast, or my favorite: a slice of Banana Oat Bread (page 38).

I find that roasting the hazelnuts brings out a nutty flavor and helps with extracting their natural oils, something essential for this recipe. It also makes peeling them a breeze. If you purchase skin-off hazelnuts, you can skip this step but might need to add a little bit more coconut oil to give the spread a smooth texture.

GF **DF** **EF**

Yield: 1 cup

1 cup (150 g) roasted hazelnuts
½ cup (120 g) coconut milk
⅓ cup (115 g) honey
¼ cup (30 g) unsweetened
  cocoa powder
1 tablespoon (15 ml) coconut oil
1 teaspoon vanilla extract

To roast the hazelnuts, preheat oven to 350°F (180°C). Spread the hazelnuts in a single layer on a baking sheet.

Bake for 12 to 15 minutes, stirring every 5 minutes or so. They are done when fragrant and skin is cracked and loose from the hazelnut.

Remove from oven. Allow hazelnuts to cool and transfer them onto a large kitchen towel. Wrap and massage them inside the towel to remove the skins.

Place the nuts in a food processor and process until smooth. Add the coconut milk, honey, cocoa powder, coconut oil, and vanilla extract, and process until smooth.

Kitchen Note

☙ *Refrigerate in a covered glass jar for up to 3 weeks.*

Edible Cookie Dough

Simple, delicious, and paired with crunchy apple slices,
this is one enjoyable treat you'll be happy to eat.

Yield: 4 servings

———

1 cup (118 g) almond flour
¼ cup (33 g) coconut flour
¼ cup (80 g) plus 1 tablespoon
   (20 g) honey
3 tablespoons (45 ml) melted
   coconut oil
1 tablespoon vanilla extract
¼ teaspoon salt
¼ cup (40 g) dark chocolate
   chips

———

*For this recipe to be dairy-free,
use allergy-friendly chocolate
chips.*

Combine all the ingredients, except the chocolate chips, in a
medium bowl. Stir to combine until a thick dough forms. Fold
in the chocolate chips until evenly distributed.

Cover and refrigerate for 1 hour or until firm. Serve with sliced
apples.

———

Kitchen Note

ᵥ *Refrigerate leftovers inside an airtight container for up to
3 days.*

Pies and Cheesecakes

Banana Cream Pie

A sweet almond crust layered with bananas and creamy whipped vanilla pudding, this Banana Cream Pie is a delicious spin on the traditional. What I love is that there's no baking required to make this dessert, so it's the perfect make-ahead recipe. I recommend allowing it to sit in the fridge as long as possible so that the filling can set.

Yield: 8 servings

Crust
1 ½ cups (140 g) almonds
½ cup (57 g) almond flour
1 cup (175 g) pitted dates
2 tablespoons (30 ml) melted
  coconut oil
½ teaspoon cinnamon
½ teaspoon vanilla extract
¼ teaspoon salt

Filling
2 14-ounce (400 ml) cans
  coconut cream, refrigerated
¼ cup (85 g) honey
½ tablespoon (7 ml) vanilla
  extract
¼ teaspoon cinnamon
2 bananas, sliced

½ cup (60 g) chopped walnuts

In a food processor, combine the almonds, almond flour, dates, coconut oil, cinnamon, vanilla extract, and salt. Process until the mixture is thick.

Press the crust mixture into a 9-inch (23 cm) round pie pan and refrigerate for 2 hours or until firm.

Scoop the coconut cream from both cans into a large bowl; add the honey, vanilla extract, and cinnamon. Using a hand mixer, whip the ingredients until thick and smooth.

Layer the sliced bananas over the crust.

Pour the filling over the crust and layer of bananas, spreading it in an even layer. Refrigerate until firm, about 2 to 3 hours.

Top with walnuts before serving.

Key Lime Pie Squares

The first time I had a slice of key lime pie I was smitten. It was 1991 at a pie shop in Los Gatos, California. While I've made many key lime pies over the years, none compared to the creamy filling of that first slice.

While trying to recreate a cleaner version of that original pie, none were good enough to publish. I kept coming back to this recipe and decided to turn it into bars.

For this recipe, you can use regular limes or key limes when in season. The soaked cashews give these bars the ideal texture for no-bake treats like pies and cheesecakes. Don't skimp on the lime zest—it's the perfect thing to give your taste buds a zing they'll love.

Yield: 12 squares

———

Crust
1 cup (110 g) pecans
1 cup (175 g) pitted dates
2 tablespoons (30 ml) melted
  coconut oil
¼ teaspoon salt

Filling
2 cups (280g) cashews, soaked
½ cup (125 ml) coconut milk
⅓ cup (115 g) honey
2 tablespoons (30 ml) melted
  coconut oil
1 teaspoon vanilla extract
¼ teaspoon salt
1 teaspoon lime zest
⅓ cup (90 ml) lime juice

Line a 9 x 9-inch (23 cm x 23 cm) square pan with parchment paper and grease the sides with coconut oil. Set aside.

Add the pecans, dates, coconut oil, and salt to a food processor. Process on medium speed until a sticky sandlike dough forms.

Spread the dough into the prepared pan and press down into an even layer. Place in the freezer for 15 minutes to set.

For the filling, add all of the cheesecake ingredients to a food processor or high-speed blender and process until smooth.

Remove the crust from the freezer and pour the filling into the crust. Cover and place in the freezer to set for 4 hours or overnight.

Remove from freezer and allow to thaw at room temperature for 5 minutes before slicing.

———

Kitchen Note
♥ *Refrigerate in an airtight container for up to 1 week or freezer for 2 weeks.*

Chocolate Cheesecake

Every cookbook author has a recipe that nearly breaks them while trying to create it, and this one was it for me. After several failed attempts one afternoon, my incredible assistant Camber said, "Take a nap and I'll figure it out." And she did.

Boy oh boy, did she work her magic! Her creation had a simple cocoa walnut crust and a silky-smooth chocolate center of which I could not get enough. I immediately knew it was the recipe to be included in the book.

  EF

Yield: 8 to 12 servings

Crust
1 cup (120 g) walnuts
1 cup (175 g) pitted dates
3 tablespoons (22 g) unsweetened cocoa powder
2 tablespoons (30 ml) melted coconut oil
¼ teaspoon salt

Filling
3 cups (420 g) cashews, soaked
1 ¼ cups (150 g) unsweetened cocoa powder
14-ounce (400 ml) can coconut cream
1 cup (340 g) honey
⅓ cup (80 ml) coconut oil, melted
2 teaspoons (10 ml) vanilla extract
¼ teaspoon salt

Grease a 9-inch (23 cm) springform pan with coconut oil and set aside.

Add the walnuts, dates, cocoa powder, coconut oil, and salt to a food processor. Process on medium speed until a sticky dough forms.

Spread the dough into the prepared springform pan and press down into an even layer. Place in the freezer to set.

Combine the filling ingredients in a high-speed blender and process until smooth, scraping down the sides as needed.

Pour the filling over the crust and place the cheesecake in the freezer for 4 hours or until the filling is set.

Remove the cheesecake from the freezer and allow to thaw for 10 minutes.

Using a rounded knife dipped in hot water, carefully insert the knife along the edge of the springform pan to separate the cheesecake from the pan.

Top with berries, slice, and serve.

Kitchen Note

♥ *Don't use Dutch process cocoa powder for this recipe, as it will make the cheesecake bitter. Store leftovers in the freezer for up to 2 weeks and in the refrigerator for a week.*

♥ *Soak cashews in warm water for 1 hour, or overnight, and drain.*

Blueberry Cheesecake

Don't let the no-bake method fool you. This cheesecake is just as good (or even better) than the laborious traditional recipe.

With a creamy, smooth texture that takes over your taste buds without overpowering in sweetness, this cheesecake is bursting with blueberry flavor, thanks to the added pureed blueberries, making it a simple yet decadent dessert.

Yield: 8 servings

Crust
1 cup (110 g) almonds
1 cup (175 g) pitted dates, soaked
2 tablespoons (30 ml) melted coconut oil
¼ teaspoon salt

Filling
3 cups (420 g) cashews, soaked
¾ cup (180 ml) coconut milk
½ cup (170 g) honey or maple syrup
½ tablespoon (7 g) vanilla extract
2 tablespoons (30 ml) lemon juice
¼ teaspoon salt
1 ½ cups (218 g) fresh or frozen blueberries (thawed if frozen), plus more for topping

Grease the sides of a 9-inch (23 cm) springform pan with coconut oil. Set aside.

Add the almonds, dates, coconut oil, and salt to a food processor. Process on medium speed until a sticky dough forms.

Spread the dough into the prepared springform pan and press down into an even layer. Place in the freezer to set.

For the cheesecake filling, add all of the filling ingredients to a high-speed blender and blend until smooth.

Remove the crust from the freezer and pour the cheesecake filling into the crust. Cover and place in the freezer to set for 4 hours or overnight.

Remove cheesecake from freezer and allow to thaw at room temperature for 10 to 15 minutes before serving. Remove from springform pan, top with additional blueberries, slice, and serve.

Pumpkin Cheesecake

This clean version of a holiday favorite has a creamy, smooth center and the perfect amount of pumpkin spice and goes perfectly with the crunchy walnut crust. The best thing about it is that it can be made days ahead of time; also, it's a no-bake recipe, so you can leave the oven to work hard on other dishes.

Yield: 8 servings

—

Crust

1 cup (120 g) walnuts
1 cup (175 g) pitted dates
2 tablespoons (30 ml) melted coconut oil
½ teaspoon ground cinnamon
¼ teaspoon salt

Filling

3 cups (420 g) cashews, soaked
½ cup (118 ml) coconut cream
¼ cup (60 ml) melted coconut oil
1 cup (245 g) pumpkin purée
⅔ cup (230 g) honey
2 tablespoons (30 ml) lemon juice
2 teaspoons (10 ml) vanilla extract
1 teaspoon pumpkin pie spice
1 teaspoon ground cinnamon
½ teaspoon salt

Whipped Coconut Cream (page 17)

Lightly grease a 9-inch (23 cm) springform pan with coconut oil and set aside.

In a food processor, combine the walnuts, dates, coconut oil, cinnamon, and salt. Process on medium speed until a sticky dough forms.

Spread the dough into the prepared springform pan and press in an even layer. Place in the freezer to set.

Add the filling ingredients to a high-speed blender or food processor. Cover and blend until smooth; the mixture will be thick.

Pour the filling over the chilled crust and spread into an even layer. Freeze for 4 hours or until set.

Remove the cheesecake from the freezer and allow to thaw for 10 minutes.

Using a rounded knife dipped in hot water, carefully insert the knife along the edge of the springform pan to separate the cheesecake from the pan.

Cut into slices and serve with a dollop of whipped coconut cream on top.

—

Kitchen Note

♥ *Refrigerate leftovers in an airtight container for up to 5 days.*

Be My Valentine Cheesecake

This raspberry cheesecake is a perfect treat for your sweetheart or a crowd. It's smooth and has the perfect balance of tart and sweet when it hits your tongue. I prefer to use frozen raspberries for this recipe because they are usually picked at their ripest and will provide maximum sweetness to this recipe.

Yield: 8 servings

Crust
1 cup (110 g) almonds
1 cup (175 g) pitted dates, soaked
2 tablespoons (30 ml) melted coconut oil
¼ teaspoon salt

Filling
3 cups (420 g) cashews, soaked
¾ cup (188 ml) coconut milk
½ cup (170 g) honey or maple syrup
1 ½ teaspoons vanilla extract
2 tablespoons (30 ml) lemon juice
¼ teaspoon salt
1 ½ cups (218 g) fresh or frozen raspberries (thawed if frozen), plus more for serving

Grease the sides of a 9-inch (23 cm) springform pan. Set aside.

Add the almonds, dates, coconut oil, and salt to a food processor. Process on medium speed until a sticky dough forms.

Spread the dough into the prepared springform pan and press down into an even layer. Place in the freezer to set.

For the cheesecake filling, add all of the filling ingredients to a high-speed blender and blend until smooth.

Remove the crust from the freezer and pour the cheesecake filling into the crust. Cover and place in the freezer to set for 4 hours or overnight.

Remove cheesecake from freezer and allow to thaw at room temperature for 10 to 15 minutes before serving. Using a rounded knife dipped in hot water, carefully insert the knife along the edge of the springform pan to separate the cheesecake from the pan. Top with additional raspberries, slice, and serve.

Peanut Butter Cup Cheesecake

Peanut butter lovers, rejoice: I've got the recipe for you! One slice won't seem like enough. It's the kind of dessert from which you'll have to sadly walk away. Oh, wait—is it just me? No, surely you too find the peanut butter and chocolate combination irresistible, right?

Yield: 8 servings

Crust

1 cup (110 g) almonds

1 cup (175 g) pitted dates

3 tablespoons (21 g) unsweetened cocoa powder

2 tablespoons (30 ml) melted coconut oil

¼ teaspoon salt

Filling

3 cups (420 g) cashews, soaked

½ cup (170 g) honey

¾ cup (177 ml) canned coconut cream

½ cup (125 g) smooth peanut butter

¼ cup (60 ml) melted coconut oil

3 tablespoons (45 ml) lemon juice

¼ teaspoon salt

Chocolate Drizzle

2 ounces (50 g) dark chocolate, chopped

Grease a 9-inch (23 cm) springform pan with coconut oil, and set aside.

Add the almonds, dates, cocoa powder, coconut oil, and salt to a food processor. Process on medium speed until a sticky dough forms.

Spread the dough into the prepared springform pan and press down into an even layer. Place in the freezer to set.

Combine the filling ingredients in a food processor or high-speed blender and process until smooth, scraping down the sides as needed.

Pour the filling over the crust and spread in an even layer. Freeze for 4 hours or overnight.

Meanwhile in a medium, microwave-safe bowl, microwave the chopped chocolate in 30-second increments, stirring after each round. Once the chocolate is melted, whisk until smooth.

Remove the cheesecake from the freezer and drizzle with the chocolate, and return to the freezer until the chocolate is set.

When ready to eat, remove the cheesecake from the freezer and allow to thaw for 5 minutes.

Using a rounded knife dipped in hot water, carefully insert the knife along the edge of the springform pan to separate the cheesecake from the pan.

Kitchen Note

♥ *Refrigerate leftovers in the fridge for up to a week or in the freezer for up to 2 weeks.*

For this recipe to be dairy-free, use allergy-friendly chocolate chips.

Fresh and Fast

Charcuterie Board

Treats don't have to come in the form of chocolate alone. My mother, who loves cheese, says a charcuterie board is the best treat of all. Don't let the impressive array fool you; these snacking boards are simple to make. All you need is a cutting board and your favorite snacks. Be sure to include a variety of colors—the more you have, the better!

Yield: 10 to 12 servings

———

2 clusters red and green grapes
1 to 2 cups (200 to 400 g) strawberries
2 Granny Smith apples, sliced
6-ounce (170 g) Brie round
6 ounces (170 g) sharp cheddar or hard-aged cheese, sliced
1 Coconut Dip recipe (page 134)
½ cup (120 g) almonds
½ cup (140 g) roasted cashews
1 cup (150 g) dried figs

Starting at the center, place the grapes diagonally along the middle of a large cutting board. Begin placing the berries and apples on one side of the grapes, the cheeses on the other.

In a small dish, place the coconut dip and set it on the board next to the apple slices.

Working out toward the corners, fill the gaps with the almonds, cashews, and dried figs.

———

SALTY ADD-INS

♥ *Salami*

♥ *Prosciutto*

♥ *Hummus*

♥ *Aged, sharp cheeses (Gouda, Parmesan, Asiago)*

♥ *Olives*

♥ *Roasted red peppers*

♥ *Rice crackers*

SWEET-SPOTS

♥ *Dried apricots*

♥ *Sliced melon*

♥ *Oranges*

♥ *Pomegranate seeds*

♥ *Dark chocolate*

———

Kitchen Note

♥ *Full-fat dairy cheeses are the exception to the dairy-free clean ingredients list. There are many nut-based "cheeses" available at the grocery; however, make sure to check the ingredients list on the label of dairy-free alternatives.*

Spicy Mango Bites

This refreshing treat is incredibly simple and perfect on a hot summer day. Start with chilled mangoes, peel them, and sprinkle with fresh lime juice and Tajin, a chili-like seasoning. It's spicy, salty, sweet, and so good! Try the seasoning with oranges, pineapple, or ripe peaches.

Yield: 2 servings

2 cups (350 g) cubed mango
½ lime, juiced
¼ teaspoon Tajin seasoning

In a medium bowl, toss mango pieces with the lime juice. Sprinkle Tajin seasoning over the top and serve.

Apple Nachos

This takes a favorite snack of apples and peanut butter to a whole new level! If you want to change it up, drizzle the apples with Caramel Sauce (page 171) and Homemade Magic Shell (page 171).

Yield: 4 servings

1 large Granny Smith apple, thinly sliced
¼ cup (62 g) almond butter
2 tablespoons (12 g) unsweetened shredded coconut
Dark chocolate chips (optional)

Arrange the apple slices on a plate.

In a small microwave-safe bowl, microwave the almond butter for a few seconds on high until melted. *Omit this step if you're using natural almond butter that is already in a liquid form.*

Drizzle the almond butter over the apple slices and sprinkle with the coconut and chocolate chips, if using.

For this recipe to be dairy-free, use allergy-friendly chocolate chips.

Cinnamon Roasted Chickpeas

A lighter version of honey roasted peanuts, these chickpeas are a fun, sweet snack you can serve to guests or keep them all to yourself! I often add them to a charcuterie board for a hint of sweetness among so much salty goodness.

Yield: 4 servings

2 15-ounce (425 g) cans chickpeas or garbanzo beans, drained and rinsed
¼ cup (45 g) coconut sugar
2 tablespoons (16 g) cinnamon
¼ teaspoon salt
2 tablespoons (27 g) olive oil

Preheat the oven to 400°F (205°C). Line a baking sheet with parchment paper.

Pat the chickpeas dry with paper towels, removing as much moisture as possible.

Place the chickpeas on the prepared baking sheet and bake for 15 minutes. Meanwhile, add the coconut sugar, cinnamon, and salt to a medium bowl and stir to combine.

Remove the chickpeas from the oven and drizzle with the olive oil. Stir the chickpeas with a spatula to coat with the oil; then sprinkle with the cinnamon sugar. Place the pan back in the oven and bake for an additional 15 minutes or until crispy.

Remove the pan from the oven and allow to cool before serving.

Kitchen Note

ⱱ *Pack leftover chickpeas in an airtight container and store at room temperature for up to 3 days.*

Banana Split Sundaes

When I first moved to the United States in my teens, my high school friends and I would walk over to a small ice cream parlor near the school for an afternoon treat. Instead of serving their sundaes the traditional way, where the banana is split down the middle and everything else is placed on top, they called theirs "layered sundaes" in which all the toppings were layered inside a glass jar.

Their sizes were 8 ounces (single), 16 ounces (couples), and 32 ounces (family). My friends and I would order a family-size jar, in which we'd dig our long iced-tea spoons and devour while sharing jokes.

This version, in single jars, is what I now make at home with my family. The creamy, strawberry ice cream paired with the perfect banana—not too ripe and not too green—topped with the works makes this fun version an event.

Yield: 4 to 6 servings

Strawberry Ice Cream
14-ounce (400 ml) can coconut
  cream
4 cups (900 g) frozen
  strawberries
½ cup (170 g) honey
1 teaspoon vanilla extract

Banana Split Fixings
2 large bananas, sliced
Homemade Magic Shell (page
  171)
Chopped walnuts
Whipped Coconut Cream
  (page 17)

Add the coconut cream to a food processor and whip until soft peaks form.

Add the frozen strawberries, honey, and vanilla extract to a high-speed blender. Cover and blend on low speed until smooth.

Transfer the mixture to an ice cream maker and process according to manufacturer's instructions. Alternately, you can freeze the mixture in a 9 x 5-inch (23 cm x 13 cm) baking pan for 4 to 6 hours, stirring every 30 minutes.

To serve, thaw the ice cream at room temperature for 5 minutes or until soft and easy to scoop.

Divide the banana pieces inside mason jars, top with strawberry ice cream, magic shell sauce, chopped walnuts, and whipped coconut cream.

Chocolate Dessert Dip

You know those fruit party trays sold at the grocery store with an irresistible chocolate dip in the middle? Those party trays always get eaten at any occasion; however, the chocolate dip can leave one feeling a tad guilty. Not with this recipe! This thick and delicious dessert dip can be used to dip fruit or can be eaten by the spoonful!

Yield: approximately 6 (¼ cup) servings

———

15-ounce (425 g) can chickpeas, drained and rinsed
¼ cup (60 g) tahini
¼ cup (85 g) honey
⅓ cup (30 g) unsweetened cocoa powder
1 teaspoon vanilla extract
Coconut milk or oil, for thinning

In the bowl of a food processor or high-speed blender, combine the ingredients, excluding the coconut milk or oil and process until smooth. Add coconut milk or oil to thin the dip.

Serve with your favorite fruit.

Coconut Dip

This thick and delicious dessert dip is perfect to dip fruit or can be eaten by the spoonful!

Yield: 6 servings

———

14-ounce (400 ml) can full-fat coconut milk
¼ cup (62 g) creamy almond butter
1 tablespoon (15 ml) maple syrup

Scoop the coconut cream from the top of the coconut milk into a large bowl. Refrigerate the liquid to use later for smoothies or cooking.

Add the almond butter and maple syrup to the coconut cream and use a hand mixer to mix the ingredients until well combined. Refrigerate until ready to serve.

Serve with fresh fruit.

———

Kitchen Note
ᵥ *Refrigerate leftovers in an airtight container for up to a week.*

Summer Salad

When I spent many summers in my grandparents' beach house, there was always what I refer to as the "hungry hour"—that time when we'd return from the beach starving, and our mid-day lunch wasn't quite ready yet.

My very wise grandmother kept a big bowl of fruit salad in the fridge to fill this very need. My cousins and I would come in the kitchen asking for something sweet, and she'd smile and point to the fridge, saying, "Hay ensalada de fruta!" ("There's fruit salad in the fridge!")

This is one staple that can be kept covered in your fridge for up to three days. And the best part is that the longer it sits, the sweeter it gets!

Yield: 4 to 6 servings

2 peaches, peeled and sliced
2 mangoes, peeled and sliced
1 cup (170 g) sliced strawberries
1 cup (145 g) blueberries
1 tablespoon (20 g) honey
1 tablespoon (15 ml) fresh lemon
  juice
Whipped Coconut Cream
  (page 17) (optional)

In a large bowl, combine the fruit and top with honey and lemon juice. Toss to combine, and refrigerate for at least 30 minutes.

Serve the salad with whipped coconut cream, if desired.

CHAPTER FOUR

Warm Drinks, Smoothies, and Frozen Treats

Few things are better than a "warm hug in a mug" on a chilly day. The simplest of things—like a latte or a hot cocoa—can be the type of treat your soul needs while you're putting your feet up in cozy slippers.

Of course, these are not to be outdone by the ease of throwing something in your blender and finding joy, one sip at a time, through a straw.

The ice cream recipes in this section are the most requested by my kids throughout the summer and any time the air-conditioning is on. Because really, is there anything better than homemade ice cream on a hot day?

—

Warm Drinks

GF	DF	EF	V	Golden Milk Latte	140
GF	DF	EF	V	Caramel Macchiato	142
	GF	DF	EF	Chai Tea Latte	142
GF	DF	EF	V	Hot Cocoa	145
	GF	DF	EF	Pumpkin Spice Latte	145

Golden Milk Latte

I remember my first Golden Milk Latte; it was love at first sip! The combination of spices with almond milk and honey was a match made in heaven. Drink it hot or allow it to cool and use it to make an iced latte, a favorite of mine during warmer months.

Yield: 2 servings

2 cups (480 ml) almond milk
1 teaspoon turmeric
1 tablespoon (20 g) honey
½ teaspoon cinnamon
Dash of ground black pepper
½ teaspoon vanilla extract

In a small saucepan, combine the almond milk, turmeric, honey, cinnamon, pepper, and vanilla extract. Heat over medium-high heat, whisking often, until smooth and simmering but not boiling.

Remove from heat and pour into 2 mugs. Sprinkle with additional cinnamon, if desired.

Caramel Macchiato ❯

Deliciously sweet, with that coffee pick-me-up we all need from time to time . . . perfection! No need for a coffee shop run—this homemade macchiato has all the perks!

Yield: 2 servings

4 to 6 tablespoons (60 to 90 g)
  Caramel Sauce (page 171)
2 ½ cups (600 ml) almond milk
2 double shots of espresso

Place 2 to 3 tablespoons each of caramel sauce inside 2 tall drinking glasses.

Fill each glass with ice. Pour the almond milk over the ice followed by the cold brew. Stir to combine and serve.

Chai Tea Latte

The perfect soothing, warm drink to enjoy mid-afternoon on a cold winter day.

Yield: 2 servings

1 cup (240 ml) water
3 black tea bags
1 teaspoon cinnamon
½ teaspoon grated fresh ginger
6 whole cloves
½ teaspoon ground cardamom
3 tablespoons (60 g) honey
2 cups (480 ml) unsweetened
  vanilla almond milk

In a medium saucepan, bring the water, tea bags, cinnamon, ginger, cloves, cardamom, and honey to a boil. Reduce heat to low, cover, and simmer for 10 minutes.

Strain the tea through a fine-mesh strainer and transfer back into the pot. Discard spices and tea bags.

Add the almond milk to the tea and heat up on low. Divide tea between 2 mugs.

Hot Cocoa

Hot cocoa is a must for cold weather and whenever you need something warm and sweet. Making your own is easy and tastes so much better than the powdery packet.

Yield: 4 servings

—

¼ cup (30 g) unsweetened cocoa powder

3 tablespoons (60 g) honey

⅓ cup (80 ml) hot water

⅛ teaspoon salt

4 cups (960 ml) unsweetened almond milk

1 teaspoon vanilla extract

Whipped Coconut Cream (page 17) (optional)

In a medium saucepan over medium heat, combine the cocoa powder, honey, water, and salt. Cook, stirring constantly, until smooth, bringing to a simmer but not to a boil.

Reduce heat to low and whisk in the milk and vanilla extract. Continue stirring until heated through.

Remove from heat and pour into mugs. Top with whipped coconut cream, if using.

—

Kitchen Note

♥ *You can substitute the honey for 3 teaspoons (15 ml) of liquid stevia.*

Pumpkin Spice Latte

If you get excited when "pumpkin spice" hits the shelves, this recipe is for you!

Yield: 2 servings

—

2 cups (480 ml) unsweetened almond milk

1 cup (240 ml) coffee, brewed strong

2 tablespoons (30 g) pumpkin purée

2 tablespoons (40 g) honey

½ teaspoon pumpkin pie spice

Combine the almond milk, coffee, pumpkin, honey, and pumpkin pie spice in a medium saucepan over medium heat. Whisk to combine and bring to a simmer.

Pour the latte into 2 mugs and serve.

Milkshakes and Smoothies

Strawberry Cheesecake Milkshake >

If you're eating clean but miss those drive-thru strawberry milkshakes, I've got the answer! This recipe tastes like those from a famous milkshake place around the corner from our house, but is made with better ingredients. The frozen strawberries and cashews give it a creamy, thick texture.

Yield: 4 servings

———

2 cups (800 g) frozen, sliced strawberries
¾ cup (105 g) raw unsalted cashews

1 ½ cups (360 ml) unsweetened almond milk
½ frozen banana
2 tablespoons (40 g) honey (optional)
1 cup ice

In a high-speed blender, combine all the ingredients and blend on high speed until smooth.

Pour into glasses and serve.

Oceanside Smoothie

After the second sip of this rich and delicious smoothie, I begin to imagine myself lying on a tropical beach, sipping this magnificent drink served in a coconut. Oh wait, I'm sipping it from a to-go cup sitting in traffic waiting to pull up to my kids' school. Sigh . . . reality check!

Yield: 4 servings

———

2 cups (330 g) fresh or frozen pineapple chunks
1 banana
¼ cup (65 g) almond butter

14-ounce (425 ml) can full-fat coconut milk
½ (48 g) cup unsweetened shredded coconut
1 teaspoon vanilla extract
½ cup ice
Whipped Coconut Cream (page 17)

In a high-speed blender, combine all the ingredients, excluding the whipped coconut cream, and blend on medium speed until smooth.

Pour into glasses, top with whipped coconut cream, and serve.

Chocolate Almond Butter Banana Shake →

One of my favorite snacks is banana with almond butter—this shake has both plus cocoa powder, which gives it a boost in antioxidants and instantly satisfies my chocolate craving! The best part? You can sip it for breakfast without any guilt.

Yield: 2 servings

---

1 small banana, frozen
1 ½ cups (360 ml) unsweetened almond milk
¼ cup (20 g) old fashioned oats

2 tablespoons (32 g) almond butter
1 tablespoon (7 g) unsweetened cocoa powder

In a high-speed blender, combine all the ingredients. Blend on medium speed until smooth.

Pour the contents into 2 glasses and serve.

Pumpkin Pie Smoothie

This smoothie is for those times when I want pumpkin pie but I want to stay in line with my nutritional goals. It's thick, creamy, and super delicious.

Yield: 2 servings

---

1 medium frozen banana
½ cup (120 g) pumpkin purée
1 ½ tablespoons (24 g) almond butter
1 cup (240 ml) canned coconut milk

½ teaspoon pumpkin pie spice
¼ teaspoon cinnamon
1 teaspoon vanilla
2 scoops (28 g) vanilla protein powder
2 teaspoon (30 ml) maple syrup (optional)
1 cup ice

In a high-speed blender, combine all the ingredients and blend on medium speed until smooth.

Pour into glasses and serve.

Matcha Green Tea Frappuccino

I remember trying a green tea Frappuccino for the first time at a local coffee shop; it left me shocked. Who knew the bamboo green beverage could both taste delicious and pack health benefits? Thanks to the matcha, this frozen treat gives you a boost of energy you need.

Yield: 2 servings

3 cups ice cubes
2 cups (480 ml) canned
  coconut milk
1 teaspoon vanilla extract
1 tablespoon (20 g) honey
1 teaspoon liquid stevia
2 tablespoons (6 g) matcha
  green tea powder

In a high-speed blender, combine all the ingredients, and blend until smooth.

Pour into glasses and serve.

Chocolate Smoothie Bowl

>

What's the difference between smoothie bowls and regular smoothies? Smoothie bowls have a much thicker consistency so you can top them with your favorite add-ons and eat with a spoon, making them an ideal healthy dessert.

Yield: 2 servings

2 cups (480 ml) unsweetened almond milk

1 frozen banana

1 small avocado, peeled and pitted

5 pitted dates

1 tablespoon (10 g) chia seeds

2 scoops (28 g) chocolate protein powder (optional)

¼ cup (30 g) unsweetened cocoa powder

1 cup ice

In a high-speed blender, combine all the ingredients and blend on medium speed until smooth, pausing to scrape the sides if necessary.

Pour the smoothie into two bowls and top with sliced bananas, strawberries, and chopped almonds.

Cinnamon Roll Smoothie

Inspired by my kids' favorite breakfast, this smoothie is much easier to make and healthy too! The oats and frozen banana give it a thicker, malt-like texture.

Yield: 2 servings

1 cup (240 ml) unsweetened almond milk

1 ½ frozen bananas

¼ teaspoon cinnamon, plus more for topping

½ teaspoon vanilla

2 teaspoons (14 g) honey (optional)

⅓ cup (27 g) old fashioned oats

4 to 5 ice cubes

In a high-speed blender, combine all the ingredients and blend on medium speed until smooth.

Pour smoothie into glasses and sprinkle cinnamon over the tops.

Frozen Delights

Chunky Monkey Ice Cream

Chunky Monkey is one of my favorite ice cream flavors, so I had to try to recreate it for this book. After all, as an author, why not put all my favorite things in one place?

This recipe yields a creamy ice cream with loads of "chunks" to enjoy from the chopped walnuts, dark chocolate, and frozen banana pieces. With every lick from the spoon, I hear my friend Sarah saying "treat yo'self" in my head.

Yield: 4 servings

———

6 very ripe bananas
¼ cup (64 g) almond butter, refrigerated
⅓ cup (80 g) coconut milk
2 ounces (50 g) dark chocolate, roughly chopped
½ cup (60 g) chopped walnuts

———

For this recipe to be dairy-free, use allergy-friendly chocolate pieces.

Place the bananas, almond butter, and coconut milk in a blender and blend until smooth, scraping down the sides as necessary, until a thick ice cream texture is achieved.

Transfer the mixture to a 9 x 5-inch (23 cm x 13 cm) loaf pan. Fold in the chopped chocolate pieces and walnuts.

Freeze for 2 hours.

Use an ice cream scoop to serve.

———

Kitchen Note

♥ *If you have a food processor or a high-speed blender, you can use frozen bananas and blend them with the almond butter and coconut milk. You'll achieve a thick, creamy ice cream that can be enjoyed immediately.*

Velvet Chocolate Ice Cream

〉

This recipe gives you that perfect milky rich texture with none of the added ingredients found in commercial ice cream. I highly recommend it topped with Whipped Coconut Cream (page 17) and a drizzle of Caramel Sauce (page 171).

Yield: 6 servings

—

14-ounce (415 ml) can full-fat
  coconut milk
⅓ cup (40 g) unsweetened
  cocoa powder
¼ cup (80 g) honey
1 teaspoon vanilla extract

In a large bowl, whisk together the coconut milk, cocoa powder, honey, and vanilla extract.

Transfer the mixture to a chilled ice cream maker and process according to manufacturer's instructions.

—

Kitchen Note

ⱴ *Keep leftovers in the freezer, in an airtight container, for up to 2 weeks.*

Peaches and Cream Ice Cream

During the summer, when peaches are in season, I love making homemade ice cream. This recipe has only four ingredients, and it's the perfect treat for entertaining guests.

Yield: 4 servings

—

16-ounce (454 g) bag frozen
  peaches
½ cup (120 ml) coconut milk

3 tablespoons (60 g) honey
1 tablespoon (30 ml) fresh lemon juice

In a high-speed blender, combine the ingredients, and blend on medium speed until smooth.

Transfer the mixture to an ice cream maker and process according to manufacturer's instructions.

Use an ice cream scoop to serve.

Strawberry Ice Cream

This ice cream is the perfect way to turn frozen berries into a decadent dessert.

Yield: 6 servings

2 14-ounce (400 ml) cans coconut cream

4 cups (800 g) frozen strawberries

2 teaspoons (8 g) vanilla extract

⅓ cup (115 g) honey

Add the coconut cream to a blender and blend until soft peaks form. Transfer to a large bowl and set aside.

Add the rest of the ingredients to the blender and blend until smooth.

Slowly pour the strawberry mixture into the large bowl of coconut cream while folding to combine.

Transfer the mixture to an ice cream maker and process according to manufacturer's instructions.

Use an ice cream scoop to serve.

Peppermint Chip Ice Cream

Mint and chocolate lovers will rave over this homemade ice cream. The bananas add nice flavor and coconut milk ensures it's perfectly creamy.

Yield: 4 servings

6 large frozen bananas

3 to 5 drops of peppermint extract, to taste

3 drops natural green food coloring (optional)

⅓ cup (83 g) coconut milk

¾ cup (75 g) dark chocolate chips

In a high-speed blender, combine the bananas, peppermint extract, and food coloring, if using. Blend on medium speed until smooth, adding coconut milk as needed.

Transfer the mixture to an ice cream maker and process according to manufacturer's instructions.

Use an ice cream scoop to serve.

For this recipe to be dairy-free, use allergy-friendly chocolate chips.

Almond Cookie Ice Cream Sandwiches

I make these almond cookies from time to time to dip in my coffee. They remind me of biscotti, except with a soft, chewy texture that's perfect for dipping. They are the perfect, not so sweet cookie to be used to sandwich a decadent chocolate-rich ice cream center.

Yield: 8 ice cream sandwiches

Cookies

2 cups (236 g) almond flour
¼ cup (60 ml) melted coconut oil
3 tablespoons (60 g) honey
¼ teaspoon baking soda
¼ teaspoon apple cider vinegar

Velvet Chocolate Ice Cream (page 160)

Preheat oven to 325°F (170°C). Line a baking sheet with parchment paper.

In a large bowl, combine the almond flour with the coconut oil, honey, baking soda, and apple cider vinegar; whisk thoroughly to form a thick dough.

Using a cookie scoop or large spoon, scoop the cookie dough into rounded tablespoons onto the baking sheet. You will need at least 16 cookies to make 8 sandwiches. Flatten with the back of your hand or spoon.

Bake for 12 to 15 minutes or until light golden brown. Remove from oven and allow to completely cool.

Place 1 small scoop of chocolate ice cream in between 2 cookies and press down.

Repeat with remaining cookies and ice cream.

Place the ice cream sandwiches onto the baking sheet and freeze until ready to serve.

Coffee Popsicles

〉

If you're in the mood for a frozen treat, try one of these coffee pops! Not only do they taste like a frozen latte but they give you a nice pick-me-up during a summer's mid-afternoon.

Yield: 6 popsicles

___

14-ounce (415 ml) can full-fat
  coconut milk
6 large pitted dates
1 to 2 teaspoons instant coffee
  or espresso powder
½ tablespoon (7 ml) vanilla
  extract
⅛ teaspoon salt

In a high-speed blender, combine all the ingredients and blend on medium speed until smooth.

Pour the mixture into a popsicle mold and freeze for 30 minutes. Add popsicle sticks and freeze for another 4 hours or until firm.

Watermelon Pops

Turn those last few slices of watermelon in the fridge into these popsicles for a fun afternoon treat!

Yield: 6 popsicles

___

6 cups (850 g) seedless
  watermelon, cubed
1 tablespoon (30 ml) fresh lime
  juice

In a high-speed blender, combine the watermelon and lime juice. Blend on high speed until smooth.

Pour the mixture into popsicle molds and freeze for 1 hour before inserting popsicle sticks. Freeze for another 2 to 3 hours.

Chocolate Fudge Pops

>

My family loves these so much that they disappear faster than I can make them!

Yield: 6 popsicles

14-ounce (400 ml) can coconut
  milk
⅓ cup (40 g) unsweetened
  cocoa powder
2 tablespoons (40 g) honey or
  maple syrup
1 teaspoon vanilla extract
⅛ teaspoon salt

In a high-speed blender, combine all the ingredients and blend on medium speed until smooth.

Pour the mixture into popsicle molds and freeze for 30 minutes. Insert popsicle sticks and freeze for another 4 hours or until firm.

Superfood on a Stick

I turned a healthy breakfast smoothie into popsicles for a treat my
kids will definitely eat! Thanks to the spinach, blueberries, and yogurt,
they're packed with vitamins, antioxidants, and protein.

Yield: 6 popsicles

---

1 large frozen banana
1 cup (155 g) frozen blueberries
1 ½ cups (30 g) spinach,
  chopped
1 ½ cups (375 g) dairy-free
  vanilla Greek yogurt

In a high-speed blender, combine the banana, blueberries, spinach, and yogurt. Blend on high speed until smooth.

Pour the mixture into popsicle molds and freeze for 30 minutes to 1 hour before inserting popsicle sticks. Freeze for another 2 to 3 hours.

Caramel Sauce

This caramel sauce has the rich, smooth flavor of the classic version, made with clean ingredients! You can use it in your coffee, drizzle it over ice cream, or dip fruit in it.

   GF DF EF V

Yield: 2 cups

14-ounce (403 ml) can coconut
   cream
¾ cup (180 ml) maple syrup
¼ cup (60 ml) coconut oil
1 teaspoon vanilla extract
⅛ teaspoon salt

In a medium saucepan, combine the coconut cream, maple syrup, and coconut oil over medium heat. Whisk until smooth and bring to a boil.

Allow to boil for 15 minutes, then remove from heat and stir in the vanilla extract and salt. Allow to cool before using.

Kitchen Note
♥ *Refrigerate leftovers in a glass jar for up to a week.*

Homemade Magic Shell

This homemade chocolate sauce is made with only two ingredients! It pours on smooth and firms up just like the store-bought version. I highly recommend it with any of the ice creams in this book!

 GF DF EF V

Yield: approx ¾ cup

4 ounces (100 g) dark
   chocolate chips
2 tablespoons (30 ml) coconut
   oil

Combine the chocolate chips and coconut oil in a small microwave-safe bowl. Microwave in 30-second increments, stirring in between each interval, until the chocolate is melted and completely smooth. Drizzle over ice cream.

Kitchen Note
♥ *Refrigerate leftovers in a glass jar for up to a week.*

For this recipe to be dairy-free, use allergy-friendly chocolate chips.

Acknowledgments

To my husband, Eric, for your continuous encouragement when I take on "another cookbook" after I said I was done after cookbook number four. You are right; I'm never done creating.

To my kids, I love you to the moon and back. Your feedback always makes the recipes I create better. And yes, Mom makes a "bigger mess in the kitchen" than you do!

Mom, even though you "don't like sweets," I'm pretty sure you're going to love a lot of the recipes in the book.

My friend Alison Bickel, your photography continues to be the best thing that's happened to my creative side. And also, thank you for encouraging me to run. You saw that I could before I took that first step. Training for the NYC Half Marathon was the best thing for my mental health to juggle all these deadlines; and finishing it with you showed me just how strong our friendship is.

Yanni, I'm sorry I could not recreate your Greek cookies and your Christmas cookies. They are both made with sugar, butter, and white flour—and I just couldn't get anything "clean" to taste the same way. I'll cheat for yours.

To Camber Ella, for preventing many recipe "meltdowns" and keeping me on track. You're amazeballs.

To my editor Amanda and the publishing team, thank you for giving me the platform to publish many of my "secret" recipes.

To all the chocoholics and treat-lovers out there, I created this book so you could get your "fix" with minimal guilt. Now, if you choose to eat the entire pan . . . I'd understand, but please don't blame me. Enjoy!

To our Creator, with you, all things are possible.

About the Author

Laura Fuentes is the founder of MOMables.com, where she helps thousands of parents make fresh foods for their families with weekly meal plans.

Laura is the author of four other cookbooks: *The Best Homemade Kids' Lunches on the Planet*, *The Best Homemade Kids' Snacks on the Planet*, *The Best Grain-Free Family Meals on the Planet*, and *The Taco Tuesday Cookbook*.

Laura's passion for helping others get comfortable in the kitchen expands beyond print into video. She has competed on Food Network (and won!), appeared on TODAY and Good Morning America, and regularly shares cooking videos on her YouTube channel, YouTube.com/MOMables.

In her personal blog, LauraFuentes.com, Laura inspires moms to live a healthy lifestyle while juggling their family and work by offering fresh recipes and practical advice.

Above all, her most important job is caring for her family.

To find out more about Laura, visit www.LauraFuentes.com. The best place to find her is on Instagram, @LauraSFuentes and @MOMables.

Index